# A Wonderland of Burmese Legends

Khin Myo Chit

# A WONDERLAND OF BURMESE LEGENDS

**Illustrations by**

Paw Oo Thet

Editions du Tamarinier

Bangkok 1984

Published by
WHITE ORCHID PRESS
487/42 Soi Wattanaslip
Pratunam, Bangkok, Thailand

Printed by Paiboon Printing.
Produced in Thailand.



ISBN 974 - 86220 - 6 - 1

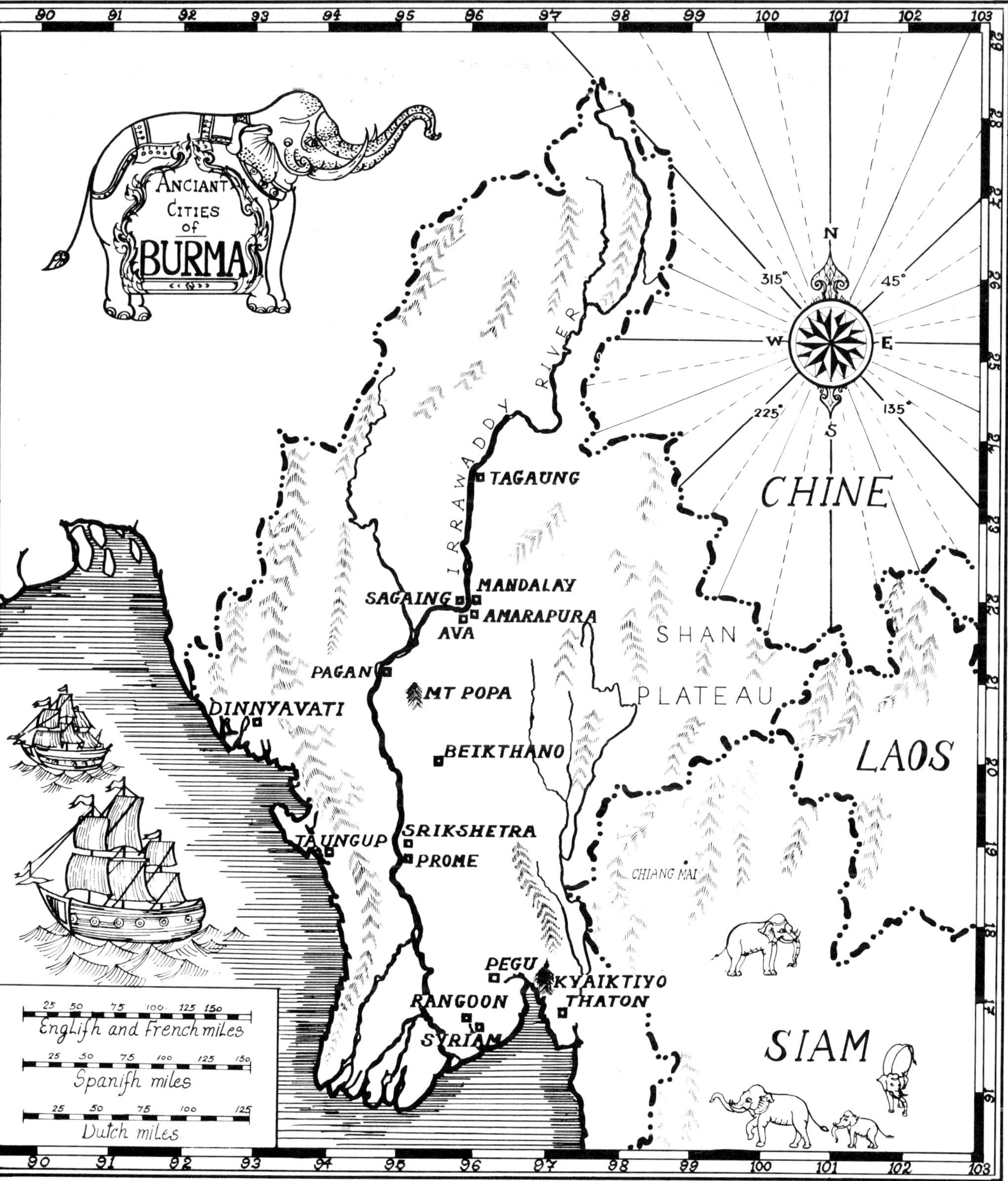

Anciant Cities of BURMA
N
S
E
W
315°
45°
225°
135°
CHINE
LAOS
SIAM
SHAN PLATEAU
IRRAWADDY RIVER
TAGAUNG
MANDALAY
SAGAING
AMARAPURA
AVA
PAGAN
MT POPA
DINNYAVATI
BEIKTHANO
SRIKSHETRA
TAUNGUP
PROME
CHIANG MAI
PEGU
KYAIKTIYO
RANGOON
THATON
SYRIAM
Englifh and French miles
Spanifh miles
Dutch miles
25 50 75 100 125 150
25 50 75 100 125 150
25 50 75 100 125
90 91 92 93 94 95 96 97 98 99 100 101 102 103

# TABLE OF CONTENTS

CHAPTER I

# A WONDERLAND OF LEGENDS

"I see only the blurred vision of colours of their skin, eyes and hair - how could I explain that these mythical beings are very much part of our daily life?"

This collection of legends has grown out of conversations with my non-Burmese friends, whose one inevitable question during visits to pagodas and temples is:

— "What do these figures of spirits, dragons and ogres represent?"

Such moments are none too easy for me. I look at the faces, seeing only a blurred vision of the colours of their skins, eyes and hair; and something sticks in my throat.

How could I explain to them what these mythical figures mean to us Burmese Buddhists? They are not just figures created by primitive imagination, nor are they pagan idols of the ancient days. They are as real and alive as any human being. They are part of our daily life. We not only see them as static things on the pagoda platforms, but also on the stage, singing, dancing and very much involved in the drama of human life.

We know for certain that these beings wander all about us, though unseen, so I invoke a prayer to them, a silent one of course:

— "O please come alive, make yourselves seen and heard - O please be friends with these people as you are with us. Please tell them, O ye Gods whom my ancestors had worshipped in days gone by, that you too have become the disciples of the Buddha along with us and that you have taken upon yourselves to be the custodians of the Buddha's teaching - that is why you all are on this pagoda platform.

— "O please make these people understand that you are fellow beings like the humans on this endless journey on the round of rebirth and that there is every chance that we must have met in the past lives - and above all please tell them that you, though unseen, share the continuity of life with us humans".

My incantation does not make the great dragon uncoil itself nor the ogre step down gracefully like a panther on the prowl, nor the figures of the celestials fly up and soar in the air. But they become alive, nudging me to tell the story, and pressing me to go on and on, and often prompting me when I strut and fret my story-telling hour, which my good friends tell me, is the finest hour. Then come the questions and comments.

— "Are these stories written down?"

— "Some of them, in Burmese, and mostly in disparate form. Most of them are handed down from generation to generation. The best parts are from the oral tradition".

— "Someone should compile them and put them into English". Of all the vanities of human wishes, I am vain enough to think that that someone must be me.

Once I began, my world became more and more peopled with mythical beings and spirits of all shapes and sizes, *nats*, as they are called, in Burmese. In Pali, the original language of Buddhism, they are called *devas*. They are also of various levels of power and goodness, as they are of various shapes and sizes. In this wonderland of Burmese legends no one could but get involved with *nats* or spirits. One has only to be in Burma for a few hours to hear the word *nat* mentioned.

*Nats* are everywhere in various guises. Things of nature, like rivers, streams, hills, trees and forests all have *nats* guarding them. To the Burmese Buddhist *nats* are real and alive though unseen. On second thought, perhaps sometimes they can be seen, if only one recognizes them for what they are.

I have very good reason to believe that these legends would never have been written down but for the help of *nats*. One of them I recognize in his manifestation; he has taken the form of an energetic Norwegian named Hallvard Kuløy. He casts his spell on me, often cajoling me out of my tardy ways - a feat no-one less than a *nat* could have achieved. Under his mystic guidance I weave yarns out of the moon beams, often losing myself in the will-o-the-wisp. I hope these legends will give the reader golden hours of enchantment and pleasure.

This hope of giving the readers golden hours of pleasure would not have been possible without illustrations created by someone who is as much, if not more, submerged in these myths. It took a good *nat* like Kuløy to find that one. He had long been contemplating on what we should do, until one day he suggested Paw Oo Thet.

So Paw Oo Thet it had to be, to play his part in this venture of conjuring up the magic of the legends. Only he who is a native of Mandalay, the last royal capital of Burma and the centre of Burmese culture, and who grew up amidst the well loved traditions of the Burmese, could have done this.

Before we proceed further into our wonderland, I would like to introduce briefly some of the characters who will be met throughout this book.

NAT. These are celestials or devas. They are of several levels, starting from those who live in the sky abodes, and to those who stay close to human abodes. This is the guardian of trees, rivers, mountains, and other objects of nature.

THAGYARMIN. The King of nats; he lives in the sky regions above. He is custodian of the Buddha's teaching and is expected to participate in all human activities that are in the cause of Buddhism.

HERMIT. One of the important characters in Burmese legends. He may be a nobleman or prince who has renounced worldly life to devote his life to contemplation.

"THE PEGU MOTHER ROYAL". She is the patron *nat-lady* of the Mons of Pegu area. Today her story is enacted in ritual feasts, the story of a she-buffalo who took care of a baby prince left in the woods. She lost her life trying to find her adopted son who was taken back by his royal kinsmen. The prince's real mother decided to wear the headdress shaped like a buffalo's head in the memory of the one who saved her son's life.

CROCODILE. In legends, animals also have supernormal powers. They too can take human form and do all things like humans.

NAGA. It has the shape of a serpent or dragon. It has supernormal powers, like taking a human form. It is considered a species of nat. Females are often featured in romances.

ZAWGYI. This character is a rather complex one. He began as a human male who practised austerities and contemplation. He collected magic herbs and concocted things like magic stones, wands and medicines. When he attained the state of a *Zawgyi*, he took a new form, a glamorous figure in flaming red robes with a magic wand in hand. The human shell he left behind was the size of a seven month old baby. It emitted a smell of ripe bananas. If anyone found it and ate it such a person would be endowed with super-strength and invulnerability.

A Zawgyi is endowed with supernormal powers, like flying in the air, walking on water, going underground. He can also create things like flying chariots. Above all, he is blessed with longevity of life that runs into centuries and what is more important, eternal youth and vitality. He is a permanent character on the marionette stage.

BILU, or OGRE and OGRESS. These beings also have supernormal powers. They can take any form and often take the human form and get themselves involved in human affairs. The females are also attractive characters in romances.

IMMACULATE BIRTH OF ETHEREAL BEINGS. For the nymphs and celestial maidens of forest and fable, entry into this human dimension comes through spontaneous, immaculate birth — from flowers, from fruits, and from the bamboos of the deep forest.

## CHAPTER II

# A LAND OF PAGODAS

In Burma, The Land of Pagodas, you will find pagodas wherever you go. Some golden and towering like the great Shwedagon in Rangoon; others small and whitewashed, on hilltops or flat lands among green paddy fields. They come in all sizes, shapes and conditions. Pagodas are not merely places of religious worship and rituals; for that matter, ritual worship has no place in Buddhist teaching. It is the human need to express devotion to and adoration of the Buddha and his teaching that manifests itself in the act of building pagodas and in making ceremonial offerings before the shrines. Pagodas are also centres of social activities. They are places for communal alms-giving at proper seasons, people contributing in cash or in kind.

Every pagoda has an annual festival, and all such festivals are trade fairs and clan gatherings. Vendors from all over the country come with their wares. Long winding rows of temporary stalls built of bamboo and thatch blossom forth with colourful goods. The revenues from the stalls are a source of income for the upkeep and repair of the pagodas.

Traders-cum-pilgrims contribute voluntary funds to the pagoda. In this way, good business is done, and at the same time, spiritual needs are satisfied. It is a meritorious deed to give away part of one's earnings to the pagoda. "Live and eat like the crow who eats with one eye on the food and the other eye alert to the dangers". This is the advice given to the lay folk by the religious teachers. The Burmese Buddhist is alert to the dangers of meanness of spirit that could send one to the lower states of rebirth in afterlife. Thus even while he is occupied in the mundane business of making money, he gives away something from what he earns to a good cause. Buddhism is a way of life that can be practised by the common folk even though they may be unlearned and unschooled'

### *Pagodas and People*

Pagodas are maintained mostly by voluntary contributions from the people. It is amazing how well it is done with only voluntary contributions. There is com paratively little or no help from the state or any other institutions. Pagodas are hence very much part of the community. Pagodas play a memorable part in the life of a Burmese Buddhist. As a child, he trots along with adults to the pagoda, where he bows down at the shrine and recites verses in praise of the Buddha. He sweeps the grounds, puts fresh flowers in the vases, lights candles and runs about in glee. He is allowed to roam freely, playing or munching his snacks. Very little restraint is put on him - so long as he keeps away from the older folk doing their contemplation.

On the precincts of the pagodas are paintings and sculptures, depicting the important episodes in the life of the Buddha. These representations excite the children's interest and they cannot but learn the basics of Buddhism with little effort and lots of fun. Adults also brush up their scriptural knowledge as they cope with the children's questions. There is a free and easy

KOH-SAUNG NAT. The guardian *nat* of all human beings.

atmosphere all round, and what may be lacking in solemnity and sedateness is well redeemed by the happy affectionate closeness created between the pagodas and the people of all age groups, and of course consequently with the teaching of the Buddha.

*Pagodas are not lifeless monuments*

Pagodas are not lifeless monuments; but they are very much alive with people of all ages and sizes. Pagodas are teeming with life, more so perhaps, than one might imagine. There are more than pilgrims on the pagoda grounds than those that meet the eye. One cannot go into the pagoda precincts without encountering mythical beings in human forms as well as in fantastic shapes of dragons and ogres.

When the culturally confused stranger asks what these mythical beings are doing on the pagoda platform, perhaps as preposterous as the statues of Zeus or Venus might be on the consecrated grounds of a Christian church, the answer invariably will be:

— "They are the guardian *nats* of the pagoda."

While visiting pagodas - or anywhere else in Burma for that matter - one will hear *'nats'* mentioned every now and then.

— "What are *nats*?"

— "They are spirits."

This answer, according to the Burmese, should take care of all the implications and complications of the matter.

One is bewildered by the presence of what he takes to be animistic symbols on the pagoda grounds, the Burmese themselves are no less so by queries as to what *nats* are doing at a pagoda. Why, *nats* are there; they have been with us for generations, so why shouldn't they be? *Nats*, like humans, are also the disciples of the Buddha. One might as well ask why there are people on the pagoda platforms. No wonder some western scholars insist that Buddhism in Burma is only a veneer and that the Burmese are animists. Others say that Buddhism as practised in Burma is mixed up with spirit worship. But neither is true.

*Who and what are nats?*

Buddhists accept the existence of *nats* or spirits or devas, not as dieties for worship, but as a class of beings, like humans. This acceptance is rooted in the basic Buddhist teaching, which is that all sentient beings, humans, *nats* and animals are fellow beings going round the cycle of rebirth.

Each being is born and reborn in the life or state decided by his own actions, good or bad. The state of being a *nat* of high or low level is just one of the planes of existence in the cycle of rebirth. The epithet *nat* covers all levels of spirits, high and low, good and evil.

*Nats* are supposed to have supernormal powers, like the power of moving at will and changing into any form they wish. It does not follow, however, that all *nats* are good; goodness and power do not always go together in the world of *nats,* as anywhere else.

*Nats* are not immortals like the Greek gods. Their life span is much longer than humans. Inspite of the long span of life and supernormal powers, they are still on the journey of birth and rebirth. They too are subject to death, decay and sorrow. They are as much in need of salvation as are humans. In this way, *nats*, as fellow beings, share the kinship and continuity of life with humans.

Because their blissful state lasts only as long as the force of their good deeds lasts, good *nats* are anxious to reinforce their good deeds. One way to do that is to take interest in humans, inspiring them to do good. When someone remembers to do a good deed, he says, 'Some good *nat* must be telling me to do this'. Humans also call upon *nats* to help them do good deeds.

When visiting pagodas the kinship

ZAWGYI

between *nats* and humans is more in evidence. The mythical figures on the pagoda platform are there to welcome the pilgrims and look after their welfare. Pilgrims pay their respects to the guardian *nats,* as they might to a host when visiting, wish them well and say *"ahmya"*, which means please have a share of the merit gained by us as a result of our good deeds on the pagoda. This saying of *"ahmya"* is important, because, according to the Buddhist teaching, to rejoice in the good deeds of others is in itself a deed of merit. When some merit-doer says *"ahmya"*, the one who hears says *"thardu"*, well done, in response. In this way the one who says *"thardu"*also gains a share of merit, because he rejoices in the other's good deed.

In the Buddhist way of thinking, there are spirits of all levels who wish to hear someone say *"ahmya"* so that they can say *"thardu"* and the good act will elevate them to a higher state of rebirth. Pilgrims always say *"ahmya"* so that all the spirits on the pagoda platform can rejoice and gain merit too. In this way pilgrims can also gain the good will and help of the *nats*. It is good to feel that one has friends seen and unseen on the pagoda grounds or anywhere, so long as one is willing to let others share one's good deeds.

Here, it may not be out of place to mention a social custom, which is widely different from that of the West. People here in Burma tell of the good deeds they have done to their friends, so that they can rejoice over them and gain merit too; it is a way of sharing the merit one gains by doing a good deed. A person of a different culture might easily take it for a tendency to show off.

Since a Burma trip means visiting pagodas, one could start with the great Shwedagon, the majestic shining stupa in Rangoon. But then, it might be more fitting to visit a smaller pagoda in the suburban area. The reason will be obvious as you go into the precincts of that pagoda, called the Mai Lamu Pagoda.

An arrangement of fresh green coconut and two or more banana bunches is a symbol of love and respect; it is an essential feature in Buddhist and lay rituals in Burma.

Specially made fans are one of the offerings made to Mahagiri ("Lord of the Mountain"), the Popa Nat who is also the guardian of every household.

CHAPTER III

# RANGOON: GATEWAY TO THE WONDERLAND

There is a smooth round piece of rock in front of that figure. This good *nat* is also an oracle: one might try to find an answer to some important question with his help. One just makes a small offering of flowers and respectfully recites a simple formula: "Please say that I shall get my wish by making the stone uncommonly heavy". One then lifts the stone to see if there is any 'uncommon heaviness'. Then, one reverses the formula and says "Please show that I shall get my wish by making the stone as light as feathers" and again sees what happens.

Maybe it is all wishful thinking and self-hypnotism - but it is more fun than pulling out the petals of a daisy reciting: "He loves me, he loves me not" !

Wandering among the tableaux of sculptures each of which tells an episode or story, the pilgrim is drawn into the Burmese Buddhist system of cosmos and infinity of time. If the story of the building of Mai Lamu pagoda dates back far beyond authenticity, a stickler for facts might be even more aghast to be taken backward into the abyss of time.

One of the sculpture groups shows the Buddha and his disciples walking in line towards a young hermit who lies prone right in the way. It is the Dipankara Buddha declaring that the young hermit would come forth into the world as Gotama Buddha, after eons and several world cycles had passed.

Even as the visitor tries to work out how many Buddhas there might be - Buddhists believe that a Buddha comes forth once in several world cycles, each cycle spanning several eons - attention is attracted to the figure of a girl, with lotus flowers in hand, paying respects to the Buddha.

*She is the weaver maid, who upon hearing the Buddha's proclamation, was so moved that she made a wish to the Buddha that she might be the young hermit's helpmate throughout his long journey of rebirths as he strove to attain Buddhahood. It is a love story that lasted millions of rebirths, until the pair was reborn as Prince Siddhattha and Princess Yododhara, twenty-five centuries ago, within the memory of recorded time.*

This story should prepare the visitor for more stories wherein characters are born and reborn in various guises all accompanied by the deeds and wishes they had made as they progress through the cycle of rebirths. This principle of rebirth, one basis of Buddhist teaching, permeates all the legends.

### *The crocodile Nga Moe Yeik*

One favourite place for children on the pagoda precincts is the figure of a huge sculptured crocodile, terrible in its lifelikeness and yet so harmless. Children enjoy riding on its back and often put their hands into the immense jaws. Perhaps it was like that in those days when King Ukkalapa was a small boy.

The figure represents the crocodile named Nga Moe Yeik, "Rain Cloud Shadow". He was not an ordinary crocodile. He was born of the mother crocodile who swallowed the drops of holy water when they fell into the seas as the messenger was carrying the cask, the gift of her celestial lover Thagyarmin, to Mai Lamu.

So Nga Moe Yeik the crocodile was, in a way, a kinsman to King Ukkalapa, whose playmate he was. If one stands up on the crocodile figure and looks east one can see a thin line of stream flowing into the Rangoon river. It is the tidal creek where Min Nandar, King Ukkalapa's young son, waited for Nga Moe Yeik.

*Nga Moe Yeik was to serve the young prince as more than a playmate. Later, Min Nandar, long past childish games, became a lover sighing like a furnace, impatient for Nga Moe Yeik to carry him across the river to Syriam where his love Princess Mway Noon waited in her lonely tower.*

*Every night Nga Moe Yeik took the young prince on his back across the river to Syriam and back to Dagon. Min Nandar had to keep the affair secret from his father, fearing his anger. King Ukkalapa would certainly not be amused by his son and heir getting entangled with a girl who was not even considered fit to be taken into the royal city of her own father, who kept her out on a lonely beach.*

*The circumstances of her birth kept Princess Mway Noon outside the royal city. Her mother died while Mway Noon was still unborn; and when the body was taken outside the city to be cremated people saw that the baby inside her was still alive. So the baby was removed alive and well, but custom would not allow one born on the cemetery ground to be taken into the royal city. The sorrowing king of Syriam therefore built a tower on the beach and let Mway Noon be reared and brought up in the best possible way. She grew up to be a maid of uncommon beauty and her father showered gifts on her and she was given every luxury as a princess, everything except the right to enter the royal city.*

*So Princess Mway Noon, with all her beauty and charm, lived in the lonely tower with no other companions except her maids and servants. Her lonesome days were over when the handsome prince Min Nandar came riding on the crocodile's back over the rolling waves; a lover of such fantastic glamour no girl had ever seen or loved. So every night Min Nandar, riding on Nga Moe Yeik's back, came to Mway Noon's tower.*

Every night, Nga Moe Yeik, the crocodile, carried his master the prince Min Nandar of Rangoon to Syriam.

... Where Princess Mway Noon awaited in her lonely tower by the sea.

*When Min Nandar's nocturnal activities came to be known by his father the king, he was enraged. As king and father he could not let his royal line be tarnished by his amorous son's misalliance with the "girl of the cemetery". So he commanded that there were to be no more trips to Syriam and Nga Moe Yeik was forbidden to help the love-sick boy on any account. Min Nandar pined for his love. Pale and wan, he begged Nga Moe Yeik to carry him to the other side of the river just once, for the last time, he said. Nga Moe Yeik could not but comply. Little did Min Nandar realize that that fateful trip was to be the last; mistrust and treachery awaited him.*

*Mway Noon, lonely and sorrowful in the absence of her lover, tried to find solace in talking to her maid, who was secretly in love with Min Nandar. Jealous and resentful, the maid planned to destroy the lovers. When the princess talked of her lover's tenderness and love the maid hinted that the prince did not love her as he should. Mway Noon insisted that there was nothing in the world her love would not do to show his love for her. This was the cue for the jealous maid; she asked: "Has he ever allowed you to lie on his right side and let your head rest on his right arm?".*

*The princess was shaken by the realization that her lover had never allowed her to do that. But she tried to convince the maid, and more important than anything, herself, that it was just nothing; not important; it did not mean a thing. The maid insisted that she should test her lover by asking that favour of him.*

*That night the union of the lovers was marred by the shadow of doubt and mistrust. Mway Noon saw for herself that her seductive attempts to lie on her lover's right side were tactfully but firmly foiled. She finally asked why she was never allowed to do that. Min Nandar was evasive. He could not very well tell her that he had been told by astrologers that he was endowed with charisma which lay in his right arm, and that he must never allow a woman of low caste to touch it for fear of losing it altogether. Great harm would be the outcome.*

*Min Nandar tried to divert the princess's attention by telling wonderful stories of his aventures on the seas as he cruised on his trusty Nga Moe Yeik's back. But the princess was not in the mood for stories. She was now convinced that her lover had wooed and won her the way most men did - without any serious intention; what her maid said must be only too true. The prince was greatly moved when he saw the princess crushed by his refusal. He could not bear to see her grief. Her heart-break struck him deeply. He could not have the princess think that all his tenderness and protestations were but the way of a man with a maid. Above all, he could not have his honour questioned; he was not a man who had played false.*

*So he consented. The moment Mway Noon lay her head on his right arm a ball of light exploded and flew away - the prince's charisma gone. The princess, however, was happy that her lover had testified his love and believed that the light must be manifestation of his faith and loyalty.*

*At midnight Min Nandar tore himself away from his love and came to the shore where Nga Moe Yeik was waiting to carry him across. Suddenly a fierce storm broke out. Since daylight was well neigh, Min Nandar could not wait; for he knew his angry father would be waiting for him. He must get home before dawn.*

*Therefore, he rode on Nga Moe Meik's back as usual and crossed the river. When they were right in the middle of the river the storm grew more tempestuous; and Min Nandar could not keep his seat; he began slipping off the crocodile's back as huge waves beat right and left.*

*It was then that Nga Moe Yeik suggested that the prince should get into his jaws; it would be safer for the prince and quicker for the crocodile to swim across the river and get to Dagon before the king found out his son's escapade. Min Nandar, already feeling low because he knew that he had lost his charisma, was shaken by Nga Moe Yeik's words. Could he trust a crocodile - a blood thirsty reptile - though a playmate in childhood and faithful servant in his mature years? The raging of the winds and waters around Min Nandar was nothing compared to the violent storm of mistrust that raged in his heart. He tarried for a moment, and that moment was not the one to be lost; he fell into the surging river and drowned.*

*The faithful Nga Moe Yeik tried to save him but when he managed to pick up his young master, he was already dead. In great sorrow the crocodile carried the prince's body back to the Dagon side, where the irate king waited. His anger turned to sorrow when he saw his son dead. People gathered on the beach and mourned with the king for the "expectancy and rose of fair state", as he lay on the pyre ready to be cremated.*

*By that time, Mway Noon had heard the sad news of her lover's death. She had more than grief to bear; the treacherous maid confronted her with the guilt of Min Nandar's death; because the princess had caused him to lose his charisma he could not overcome the danger of storm and waves.*

*This was the unkindest cut that pierced the princess's heart; overcome with sorrow and remorse, she died looking across the river to where her lover's body lay. Her body was laid on the beach where her lover used to land every night.*

*Cremation of the lovers started at the same time. The column of smoke from Min Nandar's pyre on Dagon side rose billowing up the sky and floated across the river to Syriam side.*

*While people were saying that it must be Min Nandar's spirit going to where his heart was, a clamour of voices came forth as people cried out in wonder at yet another stream of smoke rising from Mway Noon's pyre on the Syriam side.*

*The curling fumes dashed and leaped forward to join Min Nandar's spirit, forming an archway across the river - lovers united in death. The tragic story of their love today lives in stories, plays and songs; the best quoted lines from an old song are:*

"Mway Noon and Min Nandar,
Only in hereafter,
United they are,
In the smoke archway,
Over the river".

There is yet another thread of the story to wind up; the story of the faithful servant Nga Moe Yeik the crocodile, on whose likeness children play today. King Ukkalapa ordered him to suffer the extreme penalty. He was reborn as a wandering spirit. Later in consideration for his loyalty and services, the king granted Nga Moe Yeik, the spirit, the right to administer the locality around the tidal creek, which today bears his name.

*When Nga Moe Yeik was executed he had his friends go and tell the sad news to a girl named Ma Shwe Pyint ("Golden Blossom"), who was a native of Ye-kin near Dagon. Nga Moe Yeik once saw her by the river and had fallen in love with her. So he took the form of a young man and pretended to be a dealer in gems. He wooed and won the girl and married her with her father's consent. They had a young son. Ma Shwe Pyint came to the place of execution and took the bones and enshrined them in a pagoda.*

It is today called Nga Moe Yeik Pagoda and it is situated at ninth mile on Prome Road in Rangoon. One peculiarity of the pagoda is that the annual festival is celebrated not on the waxing days of the moon like all other pagodas but on the waning days; because it was built in great sorrow.

A bridge that was also named after Nga Moe Yeik was the favourite target of Allied aerial attacks during the World War II. But it was not those bombings that ended the old bridge, even though hundreds of bomb craters could be seen around it after the War ended. People say that the bridge had not been hit even by stray shrapnel because the spirit of Nga Moe Yeik guarded it so well. Those with imagination say that the spirit caught every bomb that fell and threw it away

from the bridge; and that Nga Moe Yeik was able to do so with his super-tentacles created for the job. Whatever the reason, the old bridge remained intact until it was removed to make way for a new one, bearing the same name, Nga Moe Yeik bridge.

The likeness of Nga Moe Yeik can be seen on the steps of the southern stairway to the Shwedagon Pagoda. The story of Shwedagon begins on the precincts of Mai Lamu Pagoda where a tableau of sculptures tells how the Buddha had given some of his hairs to two brothers who travelled overland to India. Now we return to Mai Lamu Pagoda. A footpath leads the pilgrim along a small lake which mirrors a huge sitting Buddha; two young men sit at the Buddha's feet. The Buddha's hand stretches towards one of them with a gift of hairs. The brothers' names, Sphussa and Phalika, live today as important characters in the building of the Shwedagon Pagoda, along with King Ukkalapa whose patronage and efforts did great service to the teaching of the Buddha.

Now our narrative turns to Shwedagon.

The curling smoke from the funeral pyres of the two lovers, Prince Min Nandar on Rangoon side and Princess Mway Noon on the Syriam shore, formed an archway over the river - lovers united in death.

## SHWEDAGON

Under the cool shelter of the gabled roof, the pilgrim slowly ascends the stairway on the northern side of the pagoda. Stretched full Length on the balustrade is the huge sculptured likeness of Nga Moe Yeik the Crocodile, an old friend. The pilgrim reaches the top of the hill where a smooth tiled platform opens out under the sky, where the great stupa stands. The pilgrim has yet to pick up the threads of the story of the two merchant brothers right there from the carving overhead.

Between the two massive pillars, a series of wood carvings hangs like a heavily embroidered drapery at a doorway. Groups of human and animal figures are surrounded by layers of delicately chiselled flowers, leaves and foliage, which fall gracefully like folds of a scalloped edge of a window curtain.

To the right is the carving that shows a caravan of bullock carts led by the two merchant brothers Sona and Uttara being stopped by a *nat*. He is a good *nat* who had been a kinsman of the brothers in their former birth. He gives them the glad news of Prince Siddattha of the Sakkya clan attaining Enlightenment as the Buddha. The *nat* then guides them to the place where the Buddha sits under the Bodhi tree.

The story then moves to a carving which shows the Buddha sitting under the Bodhi tree with the merchant brothers by his side. The brothers are offering honey cakes to the Buddha, who has not got a receptacle to receive them. Since it is not meant that the Buddha should receive the gift wiht his bare hands, Thagyarmin came and made an offering of a bowl made of stone.

### *The Legend*

*This is the beginning of the story of the Shwedagon Pagoda. The brothers hearing the Buddha teach the Path to Cessation of Suffering, were so filled with ecstasy that they could not bear to come away, until the Buddha gave them the 8 Hair relics and an important mission for them to fulfil, namely to be instrumental in the building of the Shwedagon Pagoda.*

*It was a great moment, for, the Eight Hairs were to be the making of a kingdom and an ever enduring foundation of faith that would shape the destiny of a people. As the brothers took the Hairs in their hands, the Hairs shone forth in a thousand brilliant hues that illumined the woodlands. The earth trembled with joy and wonder and the resounding clamour arose as the seas and oceans leapt forth in exultation. Mount Meru, the abode of Thagyarmin and his* nats, *bowed its head in reverence. All the* nats *let forth a joyous "Well done, Well done."*

*The Buddha's parting mandate for the brothers was that the Hairs must be enshrined on a hill called Singuttara Hill, in their own native land; because it was on that hill that the possessions of the three preceeding Buddhas had been enshrined.*

### *The brothers return to Dagon (Rangoon)*

*The brothers tore themselves from the Buddha's presence with hands raised reverently above their heads; they walked without turning their backs until the Buddha was well beyond their thoughts. The next thing that came to mind was that they did not have a receptacle worthy of the Hair Relics. That moment Thagyarmin, realizing that no man-made thing would be good enough for the Relics, brought a casket inlaid with emeralds. The brothers joyfully placed the Hairs in it. A stand of rubies was created by the Thagyarmin to receive the casket. Thagyarmin's servant Vissakamma, the architect, created a decorated pathway for the brothers' caravan of bullock carts and Thagyarmin himself guided the way as they journeyed towards the seashore where a golden ship awaited them, as arranged by the Thagyarmin. So the brothers set sail for the seaport town where King Ukkalapa had made splendid preparations to welcome the Relics.*

*King Ukkalapa was already beside himself with joy, even as he heard the news of the Buddha's coming forth to teach His Law. Such words as the Buddha, the Enlightened One, His Law were to him like the sweet chimes of the silver bells from a distant land. His heart was awakened as if some great potential he had built up all through his former lives had suddenly blossomed forth. King Ukkalapa realized the mission he had to fulfil. He must build a stupa worthy of enshrining the Hair Relics. A stupa that would stand throughout the centuries, centre of activities in the cause of Buddhism. From his high tower, the king looked towards the sea waiting for the ship to come. He had the road from the royal city of Dagon to the seashore decorated with banana and sugar cane stalks and flowering shrubs; and festoons of scented flowers hung overhead.*

*As the news of the ship's coming was announced by the sound of drums and cymbals, the king rode on his caparisoned white elephant to the seashore attended by his courtiers. The king boarded the ship and viewed the Hairs as they lay in the emerald casket. So great was the king's joy to see the beams of iridescent light letting forth from the relics that he desired to cut off his head to make an offering. Nothing less would do, he thought. The queen and the courtiers stayed his hand, reminding him that he had yet a great mission to fulfil. Who else but he, a great king could be able to discover the Singuttara Hill and enshrine the Relics? The king, therefore made an offering of his crown studded with 16000 gems.*

*The next day, the king ordered the city criers to beat the drum with the proclamation that anyone who could tell where the Singuttara Hill was would be richly rewarded. For seven days no one came forth to claim the reward. The king and the merchant brothers were greatly afflicted. They could not place the Hairs in any place since it would be contrary to the Buddha's word. Now they found themselves at the end of their means.*

### *Singuttara Hill*

*It was an occasion for the Thagyarmin's downy couch to harden like a stone. He looked down on the human abode and knew that his help was now required. His trusty servant Vissakkama and other* nats *cleared the untamed jungle around the city of Dagon, so that the Singuttara Hill stood prominent for all to see.*

*That night the merchant brothers dreamed that they saw the Singuttara Hill. At dawn, guided by good* nats, *they went to the place, and sure enough they could see the hill. They joyfully sent word to the king, who could not believe that the clearing of the jungle had been done in one night by the* nats. *It would take centuries if done by human hands.*

*The king rode his white elephant round the hill clockwise three times as a mark of reverence. He had been told by the good* nats *that Singuttara Hill was a distinguished hill sanctified by the praise of the three former Buddhas. The hill had seven names; and each name bespeaks of some wonder, like for instance, the abundance of grain, flowers and treasures. The most hopeful and cheering name of all says that bitter enemies chasing each other for a kill would be loving friends, once they came upon the hill, and that nothing prevails but peace and loving kindness. The personal possessions of the three former Buddhas were buried on the hill and they had to be unearthed, to be enshrined together with the Hair Relics of the Gotama Buddha. Again it was beyond human effort. Thagyarmin did come to help but this time he could do but little.*

*Though Thagyarmin's lifespan runs into millions in terms of human life, he had not been around long enough to remember the Three Buddhas; the only thing he could do was to make enquiries among the goodly company of* nats *who had come for the great occasion of the building of the stupa and paying homage to the Hair Relics. Even among* nats, *it was no easy thing to find someone old enough to have seen the preceeding Buddhas, and more important than that, to have remembered them.*

### *Sule Nat*

*Finally, Thagyarmin came upon four very ancient* nats; *one of them was Sule Nat whose likeness one sees on the precincts of Sule Pagoda in the centre of Rangoon, a pagoda named after him. Sule Nat was a powerful ogre in the time of Kakusanna Buddha; his daily fare was a live elephant. Once hunting for his food, he came upon the Buddha, who he thought would have to do for his meal that day.*

*Exhausted after an uncommonly hard day hunting for an elephant, the ogre was impatient for his meal. The quiet, calm human who was in front of him would be an easy prey. But he found that he could not come within arm's length of the Buddha. The ogre found himself up against someone he could not approach, let alone overcome. Not that his adversary put up any resistance, that figure of an ascetic, clad only in his worn robes of jute, and with nothing in hand but a staff. The ogre thought that it must be some uncanny power in the staff which prevented him from coming near the Buddha. So he expressed a desire to have that staff.*

*The Buddha told him that he must keep five precepts for seven years if he wanted that staff. Among the five precepts was taking life from which the ogre did not have any inclination to abstain. He said seven years was too long for him to go without food. He wanted the staff, so he bargained. The Buddha did not give in too easily. It was only after a long parley of arguing and protestations, which the ogre had to bear on an empty stomach, that the Buddha agreed upon the ogre's abstinence for seven days.*

*The ogre kept the precepts for seven days, at the end of which he became well established in the teaching of the Buddha. His enormous fangs fell to the ground and with them his ferocity. The Buddha gave him the staff as promised, but the tamed ogre received it as a relic to be revered and not as something he could use to hunt for his food.*

### *Yohani and other Nats*

*Next in seniority of age was Yohani Nat, who during the time of Konagunna Buddha was an ogre. He too was likewise tamed, and he received a water dipper from the Buddha. The third one, Dekkhina Nat, was an ogre during the time of Kassapha Buddha, and he in the same manner became a devotee of the Buddha. He was given the Buddha's bathrobe. The three ogres, now very good* nats, *commisssioned the fourth nat, Hmawbi Nat, to look after the relics. So he took them and buried them on the Singuttara Hill.*

*All the* nats *and men were wonder struck by the news. Now that Thagyarmin knew where to look for the relics of the former Buddhas, he directed his* nats *to dig a tunnel on top of the Singuttara Hill. The tunnel was 66 feet in depth, length and breadth. The staff, the water dipper and the bathrobe were discovered and brought out for nats and men to see and revere.*

*More rejoicings followed; it was not every day that people could see the relics of the three Buddha in one place at the same time. Thagyarmin brought six slabs of stone; one was of diamond colour and sheen; others were of the colours silver, pearl, gold and sapphire; they were for walling; and the last, the ruby coloured one was reserved for the final touch, the closing on the top.*

### *The creation of the pagoda*

*Jubilant days followed, as* nats *and men filled gems knee deep in the tunnel. Solid gold pillars were planted on the bed of gems; they formed a support for a gold couch. Four smaller gold couches, each with a ruby-studded couch on top, were put on it to form a base for the gold ship, which was the exact replica of the one in which the merchant brothers carried the relics.*

*On board the ship were four pavilions studded with rubies; and each was fitted with a tiered roof; relics of the former Buddhas were placed one in each pavilion. The fourth pavilion was for the Hair Relics of the Gotama Buddha.*

*The centre piece in the fourth pavilion was the ruby casket holding the Hair Relics; it hung on a solid gold pole carried on the shoulders of the figures of the merchant brothers. Around them were gold figures of King Ukkalapa, his mother Mai Lamu, Thagyarmin, and lords and ladies of the court.*

*Then Thagyarmin took out the Hair Relics. That moment the Hairs rose up into the air to the height of seven times the height of a palm tree. The scintilating beams from the Hairs surpassed all the gems and jewels. Then the Hair Relics descended again on the casket. Thagyarmin reverently poured cleansing waters from the well specially dug on the Singuttara Hill.*

*Nats and men poured jewels into the tunnel, now the relic chamber. Thagyarmin gave his bejewelled crown, and queens, princes and princesses and commoners gave their jewels and ornaments. Thagyarmin had the Relic Chamber fortified on four sides with revolving swords and spears and fire wheels always in action. He placed layers of impenetrable iron meshes over the chamber. Then he closed the top with the stone slab of ruby colour.*

*On the stone slab was laid the foundations of the stupa. The first stupa was of gold, which was enclosed by a silver one; then layer upon layer of tin, copper, lead, marble and iron were built, one swallowing the other. Lastly, the structure was superimposed by a stupa built of bricks of gold, alloy, tin, copper, iron, marble and clay, strengthened with lime, glue, mortar and plaster. The final edifice was 66 feet high.*

Today, the figure of King Ukkalapa stands on the north west corner of the great pagoda; on the South West corner stand the figures of the king's parents, Thagyarmin and Mai Lamu. Their story lives in songs new and old, on stage and in films, and in the hearts of the people.

Such is the legend of the Shwedagon Pagoda. The line of 32 kings continued to revere and take care of the pagoda. Then followed a period of neglect, and the shrine was almost lost among trees and bushes, until 300 B.C., the time of King Asoka. Among many good works for the cause of Buddhism that followed the Third Buddhist Council under Asoka's patronage was the clearing of the jungle and the repair of the Shwedagon pagoda.

Then historical records began to mention the pagoda as it resumed its former eminence as a centre of Buddhist activities patronized by Mon and Burmese kings. Repairs were made and the original structure was raised by one king after another until it reached the present height in the time of the reigning Mon Queen Shin Saw Pu (14th Century A.D.).

*Queen Shin Saw Pu*

Among Queen Shin Saw Pu's offerings was a gold statue of her likeness in her own weight, 90 pounds. This petite woman, daughter of the Mon warrior King Rajadarit, is one of the most colourful and overpowering personalities in our history.

She chose to spend her last days within sight of the great pagoda. She had a stockaded residence erected nearby. The remains of an earthwork stockade can be seen today on the open grounds on the west of the pagoda between U Wisara Road and Prome Road. The place commands a very good view of the great pagoda. It is essentially a reflection of the Buddhist spirit that Queen Shin Saw Pu should choose to end her days near the Great Pagoda. Her eventful life, which included political alliances that made her queen consort four times over, and her being Queen in her own right by sheer historical necessity, ended in peace and tranquility with the Hair Relics glowing and glistening in her dying vision.

So, the great Shwedagon Pagoda stands today looking down on the country's turbulent

The majestic Shwedagon Pagoda that is never apart from the land and people - in joy or in sorrow, in prosperity or in poverty.

history. Like a lotus blossom, it rises above the swamp and mire drinking in the cool crystal waters. It is never apart from human activities and its glory never tarnishes even though once trod by sacrilegious foreign boots and pillaged by thieving hands. It is a source of spiritual strength and it has shared the joys and sorrows of the people throughout centuries.

*The 1970 earthquake*

It is at the Shwedagon that the best side of human nature manifests itself. When the earthquake of 1970 caused some damage to the *hti,* the iron spire at the top, people from all corners of the country came forth with voluntary donations so that the necessary repairs could be made. People put pieces of personal jewellery into the receptacle without so much as asking for a receipt - most of the gifts were made annonymously. Most donors were by no means rich, but they gave with incredible generosity, moved by a sense of wonder and of the sublime.

Episodes of the past that live on to this day on the stage and in songs old and new were recalled; many spoke of the time when *nats* and men filled the Relic Chamber with gems when the Great Pagoda was first built. With the colour pictures of the gem-studded *hti,* the vane and the orb, in view for the public, the story of the gem-filled Relic Chamber of 2500 years ago was no longer a fantasy. What people now saw with their own eyes left no doubt of what it must have been like in the ancient days, when *nats* and other beings manifested themselves among men to participate in the good deeds.

Many devotees had stories of their own to tell. A lady who offered her ruby ring told her friends that she was one of the original donors of gifts for the Relic Chamber; she was in her past life, 25 centuries ago, a lady of King Ukkalapa's court; she had her statue in gold enshrined under the great pagoda, she said.

A man and his wife said that in their past births 2500 years ago, they were a pair of eloping lovers who had come upon the building of the Relic Chamber. They had nothing to offer except a single ornament, a diadem set with diamonds and done in the figure of a crested lion encircled within the semicircle of a naga serpent figure. Even though it was all they had between them, they were so moved by the sight of the Hair Relics that they offered it to the Relic Chamber. Now in the present life, they offered some pieces of jewellery for the repair of the *hti.* They said that their idyllic marriage, happiness and success in life, were the fruit of that deed done in the past.

No-one questions the truth of such stories; because in a society that accepts the cycle of rebirths and the fruits of Karmic deeds, the probability is there. These stories add more sense of wonder and, most important of all, give spiritual strength. There is always hope that one's good karmic deeds will bear fruit. It is only a matter of patience.

*The story of the old Armenian*

One of the greatest excitements in contemporary times happened in March 1968, when a news item in the Burmese newspaper Kye Mon featured an interview with a 73-year old Armenian gentleman, domiciled in Burma. Mr.Aparame was his name. He told the newsmen that he, as a boy of nine years had once entered the tunnel under the great pagoda and seen the Relic Chamber in the year 1914. Mr.Aparame drew a plan of the route to the Relic Chamber as he had seen it, and presented the plan to the Trustees of the Pagoda. The Trustees asked him to show the opening through which he had entered. Aparame led the Trustees to the North East corner of the pagoda. There a new shrine had been built, and it was surmised that the opening would be under the Buddha image in the shrine. The trustees, fearing some unduly curious people might molest the shrine locked the gate. They declared that steps would be taken to verify the gentleman's statement.

There is an opening on the northern side of the pagoda, known as the Hair Relic well. It was, as the legend goes, the well that supplied water for washing the relics before enshrining. The depth of the well is on the level of the river and the water rises and falls with the tide. It has a tiered roof built in 1870.

According to Mr.Aparame's account, he entered the the Relic Chamber with four young friends, guided by an old hermit. Along the tunnel pathway they saw seven hermits standing in a single file about 9 feet apart from each other. Then, they had to go down by a stairway that took them to a large space under a domed roof, which had not a single pillar to support it. The space was divided into 36 sections which surrounded a water hole which rose and fell with the tide. On the surface floated a bejewelled golden barge shaped like the mythical bird Karaweik. On this barge rested the Hair Relics on a bed of precious gems. The chamber was mysteriously illumined even though there was no opening for light.

This account became the big news of the day. Pagoda Trustees, antiquarians and researchers joined together to discover any evidence to verify the story. They did discover altogether five openings to go down under the great pagoda. In January 1970, a group of devotees went down and followed a tunnel, through which they could walk quite comfortably. After they had walked round for 30 feet, they came up against a brick wall. It was impossible to ge further. Some said that the tunnel might be the work of the occupying British forces of 1824; an attempt to use the great pagoda as an arsenal is on record.

Many devotees took Mr.Aparame's account to heart and did not give up the hope that one day they might be privileged to view the Relic Chamber, if not in this life, in one of the innumerable lives to come.

The story of the great Shwedagon Pagoda began with an ethereal maid of the woodlands and her celestial lover, no less than Thagyarmin, and then their son King Ukkalapa. Then came the advent of the Hair Relics brought by the merchant brothers from India, and later the search for the Singuttara Hill as a sacred place to build the shrine. The story lives on in songs, plays and paintings and sculptures. U Win Pe in his book *Shwedagon* says:

"To the Burmese people, the Shwedagon is many things. It is their premier religious edifice which enshrines the Hair Relics of Buddha and a glorious monument to their beauty of spirit which inspires loving kindness for all living beings. It is their source of strength in good times and poor. It has given them political and cultural unity of purpose and will. It has infused them with courage and resourcefulness. It is an essential base of their outlook and experience.

.... The founding legend provides a glimpse of the deep spirituality which is Shwedagon's. The history of its construction shows how men and women were inspired to memorable acts of creation and fabrication".

## OTHER PAGODAS AROUND RANGOON

But for Shwedagon and a few other pagodas, Rangoon is rather a disappointing place. A concrete and asphalt jungle with much too thick a veneer of modernism; there is but little that represents real Burmese life. It is mostly in the pagoda precincts and monastery grounds that one can have a glimpse of life as lived by the Burmese people. For that reason, going round the pagodas is rewarding.

Even though the opulent edifices in Rangoon are now encased in modern structures, life around them goes on as of old; traditions are cherished, customs maintained, and rituals revered and observed. Pagodas, however much they might have changed in form, retain their splendour and sanctity. They stand today as they have always: symbols of the glorious past.

### SULE PAGODA

Sule Pagoda is right in the heart of the metropolis. One cannot possibly miss Sule pagoda, as it stands at the junction of the city's busiest thoroughfares. It often happens that one may have lived in Rangoon for years and passed by Sule pagoda many times a day and still have never seen it properly. A case of familiarity breeding negligence. But there is something more than meets the eye. Around the pagoda are open buildings, rest houses for pilgrims. During the last few decades they have become centres of activity that makes the place a miniature academy of Buddhist learning.

There has arisen a wave of interest in Buddhist philosophy among the up and coming generation of intelligensia, who after absorbing what modern education has to offer, wants to delve deeper into the faith, which is theirs by birth and tradition. Their assiduous search led to the forming of small groups under the guidance of reputable Buddhist scholars. They arranged meets on the pagoda precincts and courses in Buddhist philosophy came to be a regular feature of their routine. On weekends the rest houses are filled with students and teachers. There are classes for all levels, starting from primary classes for school children. Friends and devotees come round organizing scriptural examinations with prizes and scholarships. All these have been done voluntarily on public donations.

Sule pagoda is believed to be 2000 years old. It was built at the time when Sona and Uttara came from India carrying the Buddha's relics with them. They first landed at the place historically known as Suvannabhumi, the Golden Land. Burmese chronicles referred to it as Raminnadesa, the land of the Mons, the region between the Sittang and Salween rivers. Later, the Mon kingdom extended to Rangoon (Dagon) and Pegu. Many pagodas in the area are connected with the coming of the Venerables Sona and Uttara, who converted kings and commoners to the Theravada Buddhist faith.

Sule pagoda is 152 feet high above the platform. The octagonal shape is maintained as it tapers to the bell and the inverted bowl.

### BOTATAUNG PAGODA

Botataung pagoda stands on the bank of the Rangoon river, East Rangoon. The locality is a busy waterfront with wharves and their daily traffic of steamers and boats.

The pagoda was completely destroyed during the war and a new edifice stands in its place. The original structure dated back to 2000 years and the relics were enshrined there, as happened in the story of the Sule pagoda. With all its humdrum surroundings of feverish activity of the waterfront, Botataung pagoda has its own magic. The name itself conjures up a panorama of scenes played by the cast of the thousands, thousands of men in colourful liveries, banners flying, music playing, as the construction of the pagoda goes underway, under the supervision of the king and his ministers. Botatuang means a thousand liveried men.

In one of the shrines is a remarkable ancient Buddha statue. It is called "Returner to the Blessed land". It is seven feet high and it had been brought back from Victoria and Albert Museum. It was one of the artifacts taken away during the first years of the British annexation of Burma.

In many pagodas in Burma there can be seen Buddha statues, bells and other objects which bear the appellation, "Returner to the Blessed land". Those who grew up during the British colonial regime still have memories of visiting pagodas, where a Buddha statue or a bell was pointed to them with the commentary: "Look, it is the "Returner to the Blessed Land"; it was taken away by the white men, who took away our king and who now rule our country. It was put in the Buckingham Palace. But Queen Victoria had a severe headache, which could not be cured by the best doctors. At last she had to order that the statue be returned to where it came from".

In spite of the questionable authenticity of these stories, they had been handed down from generation to generation. It was perhaps a way of impressing the young minds with the unyielding resistance of the spirit against foreign domination.

There are about forty pagodas around Rangoon. Some of them are right in the middle of monasteries. Monks and lay devotees see to the repair and maintenance of such pagodas. The usual activities, like seasonal festivals, family celebrations, and novitiation continuously take place in these pagodas.

## CHAPTER IV

# PEGU AND THE ROAD THITHER

The two hintha birds perched on a rock, the female on the male's back, established a tradition! - whoever marries a girl of that locality, now called Pegu, will be hen-pecked...

Pegu is 50 miles north-east of Rangoon and can be reached either by rail or by road. Going there by road is much more pleasurable than going by rail, because one can stop and see things on the way, and there is so much to see.

Pegu is one of the places which a devout Burmese Buddhist would not miss, for it is sanctified by the great Shwemawdaw pagoda, wherein, according to the legend, the two sacred hairs of the Buddha were enshrined. Here again the names of the two merchant brothers, Taphussa and Bhallika, of the story of the Shwedagon, turn up, as they always do, in most of the legends of the pagodas in this area. The merchant brothers brought the sacred hairs from India and enshrined them in the Shwemawday pagoda. Like most ancient cities in Burma, Pegu is yet another Shangri-la, surrounded by legends and mythical characters who are seen in paintings and sculptures on the pagoda precincts and are very much alive and close to the people's hearts.

On the east of the hill, on which the Shwemawdaw pagoda stands, is a small hillock, with a pagoda on top. There also stands on the hill a statue of two *hintha* birds, one perched on the other. *Hintha* is a mythical bird: the name has its roots in Pali language, *hansa*, which means a water bird.

Like the crested lion one sees on the steps of pagodas, what might have been a common water bird is rhapsodized into a mythical creature, with ornamental crests and tails, a symbol of beauty and virtue. The hill is called Hinthagon, and the story runs like this:

*Long long ago, the place where Pegu stands today was completely submerged in water. One day, at low tide, a small patch of land appeared above the sea. It was but a very tiny islet, so tiny indeed that there was not enough space for the two* hintha *birds soaring above to alight.*

*The male* hintha *bird landed first and his mate perched on his back. In course of time, the delta expanded and the patch of land became a hillock, a historical landmark.*

*To this day, people say that any man who marries a Pegu girl will be hen-pecked, a tradition established by the female* hintha *bird who perched on her mate's back.*

*The founding of Pegu*

*The terrain around Hinthagon hill gradually developed into a rich fertile land, interspersed with a network of rivers and tidal creeks, conveniently open to sea-faring peoples. The place became a haunt of merchants and explorers whose stirring deeds and battles over the possession of the land became part of the fantastic pattern which is the story of the founding of Pegu.*

*Into this arabesque is woven the episode of a young baby prince left, during the tribal wars, to die in the jungle. He was reared by a wild buffalo cow. Later, grown into manhood, he was found and recognized by his kinsmen who restored him to his rightful position in the royal court.*

*As he did not return to his forest home, his mother the buffalo cow began rampaging the countryside, destroying paddy fields and killing people, as she roamed in search of her son. The voice of the people clamouring for protection reached the king, who commanded the young prince to go out and hunt down the buffalo cow.*

*The young prince, reluctant to admit his association with the buffalo cow, could not but obey. When he arrived at the area where the buffalo cow was in full action, he did what he thought would save his adopted mother: he shouted, warning her to keep away. He would have to shoot, once she came within range of his trusty bow. The buffalo cow chose to have just a glimpse of her beloved son and paid with her life. Only then was the prince overcome with sorrow and remorse. He had been ashamed to admit that he was nurtured with the milk of her breast, now pierced with his lethal arrow. He saw the foolishness of his action.*

*No longer caring, even if his past relations with the buffalo cow might tarnish his image as a royal prince, he gave the buffalo cow a burial fit for a queen. He held a ritual feast in her honour every year on the anniversary of her tragic death.*

People were so moved by the mother's devotion and the son's grief, that they all joined in giving an annual feast in her honour, a custom carried on to this day. She became the guardian spirit of the people living around Pegu. She is today known in Burmese as "The Pegu Mother Royal"

As one ascends the steps of the Shwedagon Pagoda in Rangoon, among many objects displayed in the stalls, there will be statuettes of a lady dressed in black, wearing a headdress of buffalo horns. She graces the homes of the Pegu families, a memorial to a mother's love.

There patterns of animism are tempered with stories of how the Buddha's relics were brought from India and enshrined in the great pagoda and the stirring account of the exciting times when the hearts of the people were awakened to the Word of the Buddha and how they expressed their faith by building beautiful pagodas.

## KYAIKKALOH

There are many interesting sights on the way to Pegu. As one is well past Mingaladon Airport, Kyaikkaloh pagoda comes into view. It stands on a hill, a few yards off the highway, a picturesque spot embosomed in a grove of leafy trees and mirrored in a small lake. The legend claims that the pagoda was built in 426 B.C. when eight missionary Buddhist monks came from India carrying the Buddha's relics.

The then reigning king and his ministers were the first converts. The king, overwhelmed with adoration, wished to share the sweetness of the Word of the Buddha with his people. He wanted his people to have the fruits of the Buddha's teaching, so he distributed the Buddha's relics among them, from the high officials of the court to the commoners.

The king built pagodas and enshrined the relics, and the ministers and commomers followed his example, expressing their devotion to the Buddhist faith by building pagodas and enshrining relics in them.

In this way, pagodas multiplied to grace the landscape of the kingdom, whether in a royal city, a humble village, or a lonely hilltop in the deep jungle. People, regardless of their status could have access to the shrines, which became centres of spiritual as well as social activities. This tradition is still in practice to this day.

Even before the pagoda was built, the hill was already a sanctified spot. The popular legend of the hill was associated with an episode that happened during the Buddha's lifetime. The building sites of ancient pagodas and cities are invariably linked with events that are believed to have happened to the Buddha while he was on a trip to those places. Because the Buddha had actually set his feet on these places, they became 'the glorious spots on earth'. Kyaikkaloh hill was one of them.

*Kyaikkaloh hill was the abode of a powerful and ferocious ogre who was later tamed by the Buddha. The ogre was very proud of his supernormal powers and he callenged the Buddha to find a hiding place where he could not be found. The Buddha accepted the challenge and slipped into the ogre's hair.*

*The ogre looked for the Buddha everywhere, but he could not find him. Worn out with fruitless searching, the ogre at last had to say the password 'I offer thee flower', admitting he had lost the game.*

The ogre became a devout disciple and he named the hill, "Kyaikkaloh", which means, "Where the Buddha was lost to view". Later the pagoda was built on the hill which was a memorial to the hide and seek game the ogre played with the Buddha. The pagoda was named after the hill.

## SHWENGUNGPIN

*The Golden Banyan Tree: the Guardians of the Highway*

The next stopover on the road to Pegu is called "Shwengungpin", the "Golden Banyan Tree". It is an ancient banyan tree by the roadside and it is believed to be the abode of powerful *nats*, who are the guardian spirits of the highway. All buses and cars stop here to pay respects to the *nats*.

There is a brick shrine with images of *nats* by the wayside. Around is a small market where vendors sell flowers, candles, and incense sticks to be offered to the *nats*.

When a new car is bought, it is brought here to be blessed. With the car's front towards the shrine, the owner drives it back and forth three times. The mediums spray scent on the car bonnet, reciting incantations. The mediums get a large fee from the car owner who receives a spray of ribbons to tie to the rear view mirror, as a protective charm against accidents.

## PAYATHONZU

On the last leg of the journey is Payathonzu village, so named after the three pagodas of uniform size and shape, which can be seen on the right side of the road when coming from Rangoon. This area is scattered with ruined ancient monuments built by King Dhammaceti in the 15th century. The name of the king is associated with many of the pagodas and buildings in this area.

## KYAIKPUN PAGODA

Next is Kyaikpun pagoda, which is in the form of four gigantic Buddha images all in sitting posture. They are placed back to back against a massive brick pillar. This unusual and impressive pagoda is only a few hundred feet off the Rangoon-Pegu road.

It was built by King Dhammaceti in 1476 A.D. The pagoda is unique, because the images suffer no man-made object between them and the vaulted sky. There they repose in magnificient grandeur, in all weather, fair or foul. They are kept in a fair state of preservation. Kyaikpun pagoda is situated amidst the lush rugged countryside strewn with a large number of ancient ruins, many of them under repair. Whatever history says, legend tells a different story - and a more interesting one.

*Once upon a time, there were four beautiful virgins, richly endowed with wealth. Naturally they were beleaguered by ardent suitors, who were becoming more and more of a nuisance, as the sisters were not inclined to worldly life and pleasures. They were more bent on religious life.*

*So the four sisters agreed to take a vow of life-long celibacy and commemorate the event by building four sitting Buddha images; on each image would be the name of the sister and her irrefutable vow ending with the words: "If ever I break this vow may this image crumble down to earth, a symbol of shame and disgrace on me".*

*For some time there was peace; that was until the youngest sister broke the vow and the image bearing her name crumbled to the ground. She died unable to face the shame and disgrace. The crumbled image, people say, has been left like that to this day.*

feature in his reforms was the ban on live human and animal sacrifices at the ritual feasts of animistic peoples.

He introduced Buddhist practices among the animists. He did so with tolerance, allowing them to retain the practices that did not clash with the Buddha's teachings.

*The story of the building of the great pagoda is in itself a saga of the king's spiritual power which is more enduring than his territorial conquests. There was a long succession of crowded days, as people of all ranks, commoners and courtiers alike, gathered in one great force, guided by a tremendous enthusiasm for the Buddha's teaching. They all gave themselves unstintingly to the great undertaking.*

*Vast areas of rain forest were cleared and prepared for the foundation of the pagoda. The bustling days culminated in the triumphant climax, namely, the enshrining of the relics in the chamber, together with a cache of jewels.*

*The great pagoda has a romantic sequel. A daughter was born to the king on the day of the enshrining of the relics. She was named Rajadhatu-kalaya. She grew up to be an accomplished beauty. Her lyrics written in response to the love poems of the ardent Prince Natshinnaung are, to this day, the delight of scholars and romantics alike.*

*The words, phrases and tunes of the poems written by the famous pair now live in modern pop songs as well as in classical revivals. The beauty of the princess was celebrated in her lover's poems and the romance is heightened by the fact that the prince was several years her junior. He first saw her when he was fifteen and on escort duty to the princess on her sad pilgrimage to the battlefield on the Thai border, where her husband, the crown prince, was killed in combat on elephant back. It took Prince Natshinnaung several years and reams of palm leaves on which he scribed his impassioned verses, to win the princess's hand in marriage.*

Their love story was tragic. They had but a brief spell of happiness, which ended with the princess's death. Natshinnaung survived her but a few years. By a cruel twist of fate, the prince, a gallant lover, exquisite poet, distinguished soldier and noble sportsman, met his death on the impaling rod as a traitor. 'A noble mind overthrown'.

### *Mahazedi rises again*

Mahazedi pagoda, with its glorious past and romantic associations, has risen again, thanks to the donations of devotees, after lying in a ruinous heap for several decades, as earthquakes and vandalism took their toll.

The restoration work has come a long way. The structure has risen up high enough to have the *hti* iron framework crest on top. A triumphant moment it was, celebrated in 1982 with festivals of music and dances.

## THE SHWETHALYAUNG IMAGE

Driving farther east along the country road will bring the visitor to the famous Reclining Buddha. It is a masterpiece of perfection in symmetry, wonderfully executed to match the image of overwhelming proportions. It is said to be the largest Reclining Buddha image in the world, measuring 180 feet in length and 52½ feet in height.

### *Legend of the Reclining Buddha*

Tradition says that the Reclining Buddha was built in 994 A.D. by King Mingadhipa, to commemorated his conversion to the Buddhist faith after years of worshipping spirits and making sacrificial offerings of live animals.

The assembly of grotesque images toppled down when the princess, a devout Buddhist, was forced to genuflect before them.

*Previously, it was the custom in the kingdom to celebrate annual feasts in honour of the spirits. Before the advent of the feast, a countrywide hunt was arranged: princes and commoners took part in the blood sport of capturing - 'bring them back alive'-prizes for sacrificial offerings.*

*The king's son and heir, famous for his prowess as a huntsman, led the chase. As he and his followers rampaged the countryside, the quiet woodlands rang with the lusty cries of the hunters, followed by the whistling of arrow shafts and the clanging of swords and spears. Late in the afternoon, they decided to call it a day. It was too late to go back to the city, so they looked for a place to camp for the night. They came to a clearing, fringed with flowering shrubs. There, they saw a young maid gathering flowers.*

*It was frightening for the maid to be suddenly confronted by a group of savage men, some carrying weapons still dripping with blood, and others bearing carcases of recently killed animals, all bloody and with their insides all awry. This terrifying appearance was still aggravated by the piercing cries of live animals in nets and cages - all meant to be killed at the ritual feast.*

*The maid stood rooted to the spot, too frightened to move. Flowers fell from her hands. The prince was struck by her tranquil beauty, so serene she looked among the flowering bushes. He was filled with an unwanted feeling of uneasiness as if he and his followers were violating some sacred ground.*

*Then followed a stormy wooing and it was not until the prince promised to allow Dalla, for this was the girl's name, to remain a Buddhist and worship her own way, if privately, that the prince was taken to her father, a simple peasant. There he made a formal request for Dalla's hand in marriage.*

*Dalla became the chief consort of the crown prince, very much honoured and cherished. This naturally caused jealousy among the other wives, who looked for a way to bring about her downfall. It did not take them long to discover that she was a Buddhist and that she was performing her devotions in secret.*

*That Dalla, the crown prince's chief consort did not follow the custom of worshipping the spirit images, nor take part in the rituals, was reported to the king. He was greatly offended. He had Dalla brought before him and in the presence of his courtiers, he commanded her to bow down to the images of the spirits. So, Dalla knelt, the pantheon of spirit images facing her and the king ordering her to bow down to them. Black-robed executioners armed with swords stood around her, ready to do their duty.*

*Dalla clasped her hands and with her mind firmly concentrated on the attributes of the Buddha and his teachings, she bowed down to the spirit images. The next moment, the whole assembly of grotesque images, as if unable to stand the pure thoughts permeating Dalla's mind, fell down pell-mell from their altars and broke into pieces.*

*The king, seeing the miracle, was filled with fear and remorse for having wronged a worshipper of the Buddha. He declared himself a Buddhist on the spot and proclaimed that all the sacrificial rituals must be stopped. Dalla was showered with honours. Later, the king, to commemmorate his conversion, built the reclining Buddha image, not only of prodigious dimensions but also of sublime beauty, on the very spot where the spirit images fell down.*

### *Discovery after years of oblivion*

The great image lay for many centuries in ruins until King Dhammaceti renovated it in the 15th century. Later King Bayinnaung, the builder of Mahazedi Pagoda, carried on with the maintenance work. It fell into neglect again and lay completely in ruins buried underneath the jungle growth.

The king, now converted to Buddhism, built the reclining Buddha Pagoda on the very spot where the images fell.

It was only in the last years of the 19th century that it was discovered by accident. The recently established British government planned to extend the railroad to Pegu. The contractor responsible for supplies for the works found an immense mound of bricks in the woodlands. The contractor decided to avail himself of the opportunity.

With the gradual clearing of the jungle shrubs, the original form of the image was revealed, to the great excitement of the Buddhist community. Filled with wonder and religious fervour, they at once took steps to stop the sacrilege. The next thing was to restore the great image to its former grandeur and glory.

A discovery of an ancient Buddhist monument always has a tremendous effect on the devotees. It is neither interest in antiquity nor intellectual motivation that moves people to gather round the scene in large numbers. It is sheer exultation over a miracle one is privileged to see. The discovery of the reclining Buddha image was, to the Buddhists, a grand opportunity to give their unstinted service for its repair and renovation. Donations poured in generously. Many gave voluntary labour to do the jobs of clearing the jungle and carrying bricks and materials to the work site.

The overwhelming faith and enthusiasm of the people very soon turned the mound of ruined bricks into a thing of awe-inspiring beauty, the reclining Buddha image of today.

A huge steel pavilion *(tazaung)*, built in 1906, now protects the great image. Around the spacious precints are rest houses and other facilities. There are also restaurants and snack shops in the vicinity.

## KALYANI THEIN

Leaving the suburban area where the reclining image is, the car turns east to Pegu town proper. On the way close by is the Kalyani Thein (Sima, or ordination hall), first consecrated and built by King Dhammaceti in 1456 A.D. The original Sima was a prototype of the famous Kalyana Sima of Ceylon. Fired with zeal to have Theravada Buddhism firmly installed in his kingdom, King Dhammaceti despatched a full chapter of Buddhist monks to Ceylon, where they were once again initiated into the order in Kalyani Sima according to the Theravada rites. On their return to Hanthawaddy, the said monks brought the sand of the Kalyani river of Ceylon, and after spreading it on the present site, had the ground duly consecrated, followed by the erection of the first Sima of the kind in this land of pagodas. Dhammaceti followed it up with the construction of 396 other Simas in his kingdom. The original structure is no more. A new Sima built in 1902 stands on the ground marked by white marble pillars, symbols of a consecrated ground.

The place is of great historical importance. The inscription, inscribed in Pali and in Mon, is a record of Dhammaceti's work in the service of the Buddha's teaching. He also did a great deal for the purification of the Buddha's Order of the Sangha.

Entering Pegu Town, the car crosses over the iron bridge spanning the tidal creek, one of the means of communication with neighbouring villages, a rich hinterland. Timber logs, bamboo rafts, and huge barges laden with earthen pots, glazed wares, palm leaf roofing, fruits, vegetables and other products are seen moored to the bank.

## SHWEMAWDAW PAGODA

Taking the road straight east brings the visitor to the foot of the hill where the Shwemawdaw Pagoda stands. The original construction is ascribed to the merchant brothers who brought the hair relics from India during the Buddha's life time, which is 25 centuries ago.

In 840, Kings Thamala and Wimala, founders of the Pegu kingdom, raised the height of the original stupa to 88 feet. Successive kings carried on with the work of repairing, renovating and enlarging the pagoda. In 1796, King Bodawpaya raised it to the height of 297 feet.

The pagoda was shattered by three major earthquakes in 1912, 1917 and 1930. A great part of the bell-shaped dome and its superstructure tumbled down, and the terraces were damaged in the last tremor.

The great pagoda lay in ruins until after the Second World War. The State and the public then made earnest efforts to restore the pagoda. It was completed in 1954. The model is slightly different from the past: the height today is 375 feet, taller than Shwedagon in Rangoon.

Several ancient Buddha images of stone and bronze were discovered from the ruined sectors of the pagoda and they are now exhibited in the museum on the pagoda platform.

The Shwemawdaw festival is held annually in April of each year.

### *Remains of the old city*

Going down the stairs on the eastern side of the great pagoda, the visitor can see the remains of the old moat that once encircled the city, now a narrow canal covered with water hyacinth. The iron bridge over the old moat is the beginning of a pleasant path that leads to the foot of Hinthagon hill, where the history of Pegu began with the two hintha birds landing on the small patch of land amidst the sea - that patch of land, now a hill.

## HINTHAGONE PAGODA

On top of the hill is a pagoda and the story of Pegu is told in the sculptured figures of the two hintha birds, one perched on the other's back. This legend of the founding of Pegu is told at the beginning of this chapter. There are also some paintings done quite recently to represent the early history of Pegu, the landing of the two hintha birds, the coming of the sea farers and their fights over the possession of the land.

With the gradual expansion of the Irrawaddy-Sittang deltaic area, the little spot assumed the form of a hillock, and came to acquire some historical as well as religious importance. It was on this hillock that the Reverend U Khanti, the hermit-architect of Mandalay Hill and Shwesettaw pagodas, built the present pagoda with contributions from the general public. The hillock has come to be known as Hinthagone, the roosting place of the two mythical birds, and forms an important historical landmark. It commands a panoramic view of the surrounding areas.

CHAPTER V

# PROME AND SRIKSHETRA

According to the legend, Shwenattaung pagoda was built about the same time as the Shwesandaw and Pho-oo-taung Pagodas; that is, the time when the Buddha proclaimed the future glory of Srikshetra city. The Buddha, in his great love and compassion for all sentient beings, did not limit his sojourn to places like Pho-oo-taung, the habitat of the celestials.

*One day, he turned his steps towards the place where the town, Shwe-taung stands. There was, in those times, a small settlement of refugees from the north, who had run away from tribal wars. Before the advent of the Buddha, the people worshipped the hill, called the Golden Hill (Shwe-taung), believing that a great spirit was enthroned there. They celebrated a ritual feast in his honour every year in March.*

*It was during the festival that the Buddha stood on top of the hill; his aura streamed forth and the woods and the hill became steeped in thousands of irridescent beams. The whole place echoed with the sweet music of birds, who warbled their native wood-note wild, in the sheer ecstasy of being in the presence of the Buddha. The people, celebrating the ritual feast, at first thought that it must be the great spirit of the Golden Hill showing up to them in person. They were so filled with wonder at what they saw that they prostrated themselves in reverence.*

*Only when they heard the Buddha speak did they realize that it was someone even far, far greater than the spirit of the hill. They became established in the Buddha's teaching.*

*The people became such ardent devotees that they could not bear the imminence of the Buddha's departure. They made a lifelike statue so that they could pay their respects. Later, they thought it wiser to build a pagoda on top of the hill and enshrine the statue in there, so that it would be safe from vandals and such dangers. The Buddha gave them hair relics to be enshrined in the pagoda.*

The pagoda is called Shwenattaung after the hill on which it stands. Legends say that the kings of Srikshetra had maintained and renovated the structure. The earliest record dates back to 1281, when the pagoda was raised to a height of 66 feet.

The events that led to this auspicious occasion were bizarre. The once glorious kingdom of Pagan was destroyed by the forces of Kublai Khan, and the then reigning Pagan King and his army retreated down the Irrawaddy. At that time the king's son had consolidated a stronghold at Prome.

*The king's hope of finding a refuge in his son's protection was never to be. On his arrival at Prome his barge was surrounded by armed men led by his son, who was determined to kill him. Before his death, the king made a last request that his jewels should be employed to renovate the Shwenattaung pagoda. It was within sight of the pagoda that he was killed.*

The patricidal son fulfilled his father's last wish and raised the original structure to the height of 66 feet.

In the 16th century, Tabin-shwe-hti, king of Toungoo, gilded the pagoda. He was at that time engaged in building a united kingdom. This involved him in much tribal strife and the place where Shwetaung and Prome stand today was the scene of many riverine engagements. The king's act of gilding the Shwenattaung pagoda is probably a celebration of one of these riverine victories.

In 1874, Uparaja, the son of King Bodawpaya who ruled Burma from 1784 to 1819, was on his way back from a campaign in Arakan. He was the one who brought back the Mahamayatmuni Buddha statue, now in Mandalay, from Arakan. He gilded the Shwenattaung Pagoda and built many shrines and rest houses in its precincts.

Shwenattaung Pagoda's involvement in the country's turbulent history goes on and on. There is a monument commemmorating the separation of Burma from India in 1937, when Burma was given a new constitution by the British government. Being only 120 feet high, it is smaller in size than Shwesandaw, but its sublime beauty is breath-taking. The pagoda rises on top of the hill overlooking the deciduous woodlands, whose circular crenate leaves spiral up the hill in tiers of golden flounces in March, the festival time. No wonder the ancient people worshipped the hill as the Golden Hill.

## NEIKBEINDA : A RETREAT AMONG THE HILLS

There miles north of Prome is a ridge of hills with thickly wooded ridges and glens wherein monasteries and nunneries lie half-hidden. When dappled dawn has scarce arisen, there come out of the shrubby glades, yellow robed monks in twos and threes. They have black alms bowls cradled in their arms. As they walk on with downcast eyes, lay folk come out with alms food as if out of nowhere.

The monks stop only for a moment to receive the offering and walk on in silence. The lay folk stay on to wait for other groups to come their way. It is merely for a few moments and then they all melt away; the woodland is empty but for the soft beams of morning sun. It is as if the monks and the lay folk have never been there at all. This place, called Neikbeinda Retreat, can be reached by a somewhat rough country road. This retreat offers the devotees of Prome occasional peace and quiet, away from the stress of their workaday lives. People from other towns often come and stay there for spiritual as well as physical repose.

Neikbeinda Retreat, in its quiet way, is a centre of religious activity. On the days of Buddhist observances, such as the Buddha's Nativity in May, people from Prome town come here to celebrate, with the usual alms-giving to the reverend *sangha*.

## MINGYI-TAUNG : WHERE THE STORY OF SRIKSHETRA BEGAN

Down south of Prome along the river is a ridge of hills with grottos and monastic retreats. This place is called "Mingyi-taung" ("Hill of Kings"). It is a special place for the Burmese, because it was here that the events leading to the founding of the city of Srikshetra began.

Among the hills, there is a grotto, called Beydayi Grotto, named after the girl who was destined to play an important role in the history of the city.

*Beydayi was only a small child when she was found by the hermit living in the hills. The hermit picked her up and raised her as his own child. She grew up to be a beautiful maiden. The hermit then thought it unseemly to have her around the whole day.*

*So he devised a plan to keep her away from the grotto which was the hermitage. He gave her a huge gourd shell with a tiny hole at the top and told her to go down to the river and fetch water. The plan worked. Beydayi went down to the riverside and dipped the gourd shell in the water and waited for it to fill, and not surprisingly, it took the whole day. She came back to the grotto late in the afternoon.*

Today the toy shops on the steps of the pagodas sell small gourd shells each with a tiny hole on top. Encased in woven cane work and fitted with slingloops, they make attractive playthings for the young and not so young. It is supposed to be the replicas of the shell Beydayi used in those ancient times.

The hermit found a baby girl in the woods. So great was his love and compassion that milk flows from his fingers.

The grotto, now called Beydayi Grotto, has sculptures representing the daily life of the hermit and the girl. There is a narrow gully, now blocked, which people say, used to be open down to the riverside, and that it was the subterranean pathway the girl took daily to the river.

This story often comes to life in plays, poems and songs and in decorative motifs on lacquerware and silverware. The scene where the girl meets the two princes floating down on a raft on the river is a favourite with artists. Of course, the girl must meet someone to break her monotonous routine.

*Love that comes a long way*

The thread of romance that comes into the story of Beydayi and her gourd shell began in the old city of Tagaung up north, an ancient site which many Burmese today claim as the cradle of Burmese History.

*The story of the two blind princes Maha Tambawa and Culasa Tambawa began at Tagaung, the legendary Burmese capital on the Irrawaddy river up north. The kingdom was ruled by a Queen who had a lover, a fire-breathing Naga prince. He took the form of a young man and visited the Queen every night. The Queen's lover would not have any rival. All attempts to marry the Queen and seize the throne were foiled. Finally a brave and clever man came forth and killed the Naga prince with a stratagem. He put a stem of a banana tree on the queen's couch and hid himself behind the arras holding a sword. When the Naga prince came, he was enraged to find someone lying in the Queen's bed. So he resumed his Naga form and struck the interloper with his mighty fangs. The fangs sank into a banana stem, and before he could free himself the hero came out and cut him to pieces with his sword.*

*So Maung Pauk Kyine, this being the name of the hero, became King and married the Queen, who could not get over the loss of her Naga lover. She had her servants make the skin of the Naga into pillows and mattresses and cushions. The powerful scent of the Naga's body was such that her twin sons were born blind. The young princes were unwelcome reminders of the Queen's love affair, and they were also considered unworthy to be heirs of the throne. So they were put on a raft and floated down the river.*

The queen had a lover, a fire-breathing naga who took the form of a handsome prince. He suffered no rival until he was killed by a brave man who seized the kingdom and made the queen his consort.

*Fortunately for Beydayi, the princes, when they reached Prome, had already regained their eyesight, an event which brings yet another yarn into the main plot, as follows:*

*It so happened that the raft on which the two princes were riding got caught in the branches of a flowering acacia tree at a place where today the old town Sagaing stands, on the west bank of the river. Sagaing is joined today to Mandalay by the Ava bridge. People say that it was how the town got the name Sagaing (pronounced "Sit-kaing") which means "Bending Acacia Tree".*

*While the two princes were having their meal, they became conscious of an extra pair of hands. They immediately got hold of the offending limb and demanded whose it was. Instead of a formidable enemy, it was a nymph who had seen them from her flowery perch on the acacia tree. She had playfully trapped the raft in the branches, and made her presence known by sharing their meal. She had a knowledge of herbs, so she offered to cure the princes of their affliction.*

*The princes took the nymph with them as they floated down south. Under her treatment the princes regained their eyesight. By that time the younger prince and the nymph had become lovers. When they came to the place where now the town of Magwe stands, they had to leave the nymph; for she was enceinte and her time was near.*

*As for the two princes, as sons of a royal house they had a mission to fulfil, that is to search for new lands and to found a kingdom. So they went on their way, leaving the nymph. The younger prince of course made promises, the usual ones men make to girls they meet on the way.*

**Now to Beydayi**

*The next stop was where they met Beydayi at her daily vigil by the riverside. This time, the elder prince sprang to action even before the younger brother knew what was happening. He went to the girl and asked her what in the world she was doing with a huge gourd shell. The girl answered she was only trying to get water. What a stupid thing to do, the prince said. So saying he broke open the gourd shell with his trusty sword.*

*That day Beydayi came back to the grotto much earlier than usual. The hermit demanded an explanation. Hearing from girl what had happened the hermit told her to bring the princes to him, so the two princes presented themselves before the hermit, who saw that they were no mean persons but sons of a royal house. The elder prince asked the hermit for Beydayi's hand in marriage. They were duly married, but the prince died shortly after. So, Beydayi was given to the younger prince. They had a son, Duttabaung, a man destined to greatness.*

**THE FOUNDING OF SRIKSHETRA**

*Duttabaung, the son of Beydayi and the younger prince of Tagaung was destined to be the founder of Srikshetra city, according to the legends, about 2400 years ago. Now, the celestials who had heard the Buddha's prophecy, were still living, their life span being much longer than that of the humans. They took it to be their sacred duty to help Duttabaung to build the city and to fulfil the promise of prosperity and the flourishing of the Buddha's teaching.*

*All the spirits led by Thagyarmin, the king of the celestials, came round to help Duttabaung build the royal city. Thagyarmin drew the city plan by standing right in the middle of the site as a huge dragon slithered round pulling a rope to draw a circle.*

Archaeological discoveries indicate the existence of a Pyu city, Srikshetra, five miles south of Prome. The Pyus were early immigrants into Burma and they had already settled in the central part of the country by the beginning of the Christian era. Archaeological evidence indicates that Srikshetra attained its height of prosperity between 500 AD and 900 AD.

Excavations reveal the ancient city to be roughly circular in shape, the circumference being eight miles and a half. Some sections of the massive walls built of large baked bricks stand today to a height of 15 feet. Excavations and explorations around the city yielded valuable anti-

ques, revealing close contact with South India. Some of them are now in the museum site in Hmawza village. Some are in the National Museum in Rangoon. A number of large and important temples and pagodas are still intact.

The earliest inscriptions in Burma are found at Srikshetra. Some readable and datable inscriptions suffice to establish the fact that Theravada Buddhism was flourishing in Srikshetra.

## A RIVAL KINGDOM : BEIKTHANO CITY

Now the story of King Duttabaung of Srikshetra picks up a loose thread, which was left untied, when Duttabaung's father left his mistress, the forest nymph who had cured his and his brother's blindness.

*In the course of time, the nymph bore a daughter named Panhtwar. She was destined to be a great queen; she was loved by the celestials of the place, who later helped her found a city named Vishnu, or Beikthano as the Burmese called it.*

Beikthano city came out of the veils of legend and myth when excavations around ruins lying some twelve miles west of Taungdwingyi in Magwe district revealed the existence of yet another ancient Pyu city, a contemporary of Srikshetra.

Remains of the immense fortifications and objects of antiquity, coins, urns and other artifacts bespeak the greatness that was once Beikthano. They also establish that links existed between the city and Srikshetra, and that the Beikthano civilization probably pre-dates Srikshetra. Beikthano, as the excavated remains indicate, stood on a higher ground, 330 feet above sea level, overlooking the fertile plains irrigated by streams which eventually flow into the Irrawaddy.

The city could wield considerable power over the plain from its strategic position on a western outlet towards the water highway, the Irrawaddy. Beikthano, with its rich fertile hinterland was right on the India-China overland trade route. Its vicinity was convenient for merchants and adventurers to go down south to the sea by the river Irrawaddy. The prosperity and the power of Beikthano city, being a potential rival to Srikshetra, is seen in the nucleus of facts.

*The legend says that the power of Duttabaung grew, as it certainly would while he was situated in rich fertile plains and lush forest lands. Many states and settlements came under his rule.*

*Only the city of Beikthano stood defiant, ruled by the proud queen Panhtwar, his own half-sister, the daughter of the nymph whom his father loved and deserted.*

*Duttabaung made many attempts to bring the city under his power, but he failed. A ridge of hills rising up to 750 feet runs between the river and the city itself. Down that ridge, the area of approach towards the city was a labyrinth of streams and rivulets with their unpredictable ways meandering in all directions. This was a natural protection against any hostile approach.*

As excavation reveals today, the rhombus-shaped city had formidable walls built of large baked bricks. The gateways gradually curve inwards. The arms and ramparts on either side of the entrance passage extended to about 86 feet.

There are traces of a well-planned interior. Residential areas with the palace and houses, religious edifices and monasteries, and the irrigated agricultural grounds with lakes and canals; all these are found to be carefully worked out, each in its own sector.

The archaeological discoveries point out the possibility that the city would have been well provided with food and water, an adequate support in times of long sieges.

*Duttabaung was determined to subjugate the city and its proud queen. When his attempts failed he resorted to machiavellian tactics, of espionage and sabotage. At long last it paid off. He sacked the city and brought the proud queen to Srikshetra and made her his consort.*

The King of Srishetra was known as "The One with Three Eyes," the coil of silver hair on his brow making the third eye. He lost his charisma when the Queen of Beikthano, whose city he conquered, introduced three black lines on the train of her sarong and called them "eyes".

*Charred remains of the wooden gates, rusted iron sockets and crumpled walls standing to a height of 15 feet today are a silent testimony of the city's fate in the lands of the besiegers.*

*The Queen's Revenge*

*Now came the tragic sequel. Queen Panhtwar could not forgive Duttabaung for the shame and humiliation he had brought on her. Though loved and cherished she could not accept the status of a queen consort - she, who once ruled over a powerful, prosperous city, a queen in her own right. She thought of ways and means of taking her vengeance.*

*It so happened that the king had a long silvery hair in the middle of his forehead. This strand of hair curled up into a small coil which shone like a jewel. It was believed that this coil of hair was the king's charisma and that the king's power lay in there. The king was called 'the King with Three Eyes', the coil of hair making the third eye.*

*The queen devised a plan, a very ingenious plan it was. She stitched three black lines on the train of her skirt and called them 'eyes'. Other ladies followed the royal fashion. So the three eyes, the symbol of the king's power and mystique, became but a trimming on women's skirts.*

*From that time on, the king became an object of ridicule. People came to regard him with contempt. He no longer had the power to rule over his subjects. He died very shortly, a broken man. The queen met her death at the hands of the king's friends, who wreaked their vengeance on her, an alien woman whom they had mistrusted and resented.*

These personalities and events, though beyond authentication, are very much alive. They often penetrate the mists of legend with tremendous force and vividness in songs, poems and plays. There are many places which still bear the mark of their eventful history.

Near Shwetaung, there are villages with strange names which people say were so named to commemorate a royal visit of King Duttabaung and his queen Panhtwar. There is not a pagoda in the neighbourhood that does not have a legend of being visited by King Duttabaung and Queen Panhtwar, who are listed to be the donors of jewels for the relic chamber and other shrines.

And one more thing survives. The eyes or the three black lines are still seen today on the train of the richly embroidered wrap-around, which makes up the ensemble of a Burmese lady's ceremonial dress, usually worn by brides and prima donnas doing classical dances. The three black lines still bear the name 'eyes' as named by the proud Queen of bygone days.

The symbol of the vanquished queen's vengeance lives today on the train of the sarong worn by dancing girls.

**BEIDAYI**

The great hermit the father
to send the daughter away the whole day long
makes her carry the stream water
in a brown gourd water won't get in.

Father's orders!
nothing to be trifled with.
Young Beida goes out every day
days in days out days pass by.
'Why such poor lot?'
perhaps she wonders.

Has fortune smiled on her?
The Thambawa brothers come
out of the blue their raft puts in.......
the way this child of nature meets her love,
this sweet young girl Beida:
This legend of gourd and its enlarging
I've heard it told

But
I feel the truth in the tale
I long to see it happen in life and
I make it out in my imagination
how the elder Thambawa
would take the gourd from her
and with his sword's point all at once
would push and turn and make big the hole
while all the time the girl Beida
her face glittering with blushes
how she would look away to smile.......
And how I'd love to see it.

Htin Lin
*Translated by* Maung Tha Noe

CHAPTER VI

# AROUND MANDALAY

*The last royal seat*

To the Burmese, Mandalay, the last royal seat of Burmese kings before the British annexation in 1885, is a place of poignant memories. There, during the colonial days, children grew up in a community of genteel families, whose associations with the Burmese royalty was still fresh in their hearts, and who had not quite shaken off the pride of an independent sovereign people.

The royal palace, - destroyed during the last days of World War II - with its moat and turretted walls, had stood a silent and yet eloquent reminder of the sovereignty the country had lost. A well-known pop song of those days featured the royal palace as 'the one and only thing left for us to see', a note of sadness tinged with lost glory.

Old classical songs in praise of the royal city with accompaniment of music, as an item of entertainment, have remained to this day a thing of elegance and taste.

Nowadays, as in the past, people from all over Burma look up to Mandalay in all things Burmese - religious studies, cultural life, music and songs, dance and drama, and handicrafts. Mandalayans consider themselves the most Burmese in their way of life, social customs and family traditions. Alien culture, mercifully, has not affected them as it has in Rangoon, an almost cosmopolitan city.

A trip to Mandalay is a mixture of national sentiment, religious fervour and an education in fine arts. Non-Burmese visitors often feel the subtle difference in manners, speech and way of life in Mandalay, which remains provincial in the best sense of the word: people are polite, courteous, friendly and willing to help; and many have proud aristocratic bearing, as most of them have some claim or the other to be associated with the Burmese royal court, and they are fiercely proud of their roots.

*Beginnings: Mandalay Hill*

The story of Mandalay begins with Mandalay Hill, and dates back to the time when the Buddha was teaching his Dhamma in Majimadesa, as the location was mentioned in Buddhist stories.

*The Buddha, in his great compassion, often travelled to faraway lands so that all sentient beings should benefit from his teaching. On one of his trips, he stood on top of Mandalay Hill and pronounced to his disciples that a great city would arise nearby and that at the selfsame place his teaching would flourish.*

*When the Buddha said those words, all the devas (celestials) of the area rejoiced over the glad news. Woodlands rang with their jubilation as they sang hymns in praise of the Buddha. Amidst the happy celebration, an ogress named Canda Mukhi was so overcome by the sublime glory of the Buddha and the mellifluous cadence of his voice that she was filled with a desire to offer something to the Great One.*

*However, she was at a loss to find anything worthy to offer; so without another thought, she plucked off her breasts and laid them reverently at the Buddha's feet. The Buddha blessed her for her devotion and said that she would be reborn, in a future existence, a prince who would be the founder and ruler of the city which was to be.*

One of the sculpture groups on Mandalay Hill represents the Buddha proclaiming the great future of Mandalay city. The life size statue of the ogress Canda Mukhi is also there; she has her severed breasts in her hands about to be laid at the Buddha's feet.

Just a few steps away is a group of ogres paying respects to the Buddha. Among the Buddha's devotees are figures of a king and a hunter attended by a pack of hounds; there is also a congregation of monks - all this seems to show what a motley crowd the Buddha's followers must be.

*Founder of Mandalay City*

King Mindon, who founded Mandalay city from 1857 to 1859, is believed to be the reincarnation of the ogress Canda Mukhi, as her likeness on the Mandalay Hill testifies today. King Mindon is noted for his many acts of piety and magnanimity. With the two coastal strips, the Tenasserim and Arakan, and the Delta area in the hands of the British, the shadow of the Union Jack was already lengthening towards the north.

Prince Kanaung, the king's brother, made brave attempts to introduce modern sophisticated methods and equipment into warfare and industries. Unfortunately, his untimely death at the hands of assassins during a palace coup put a temporary end to the Burmese dreams of gradual modernization, solidarity amd preservation of sovereignty.

Notwithstanding the final overthrow of the Burmese monarchy in 1885, during the time of King Thibaw, King Mindon's son and successor, it must be noted that the auspicious beginnings of the city were followed by no less auspicious events in the succeeding years.

One great work King Mindon had done was the convening of the Fifth Buddhist Synod. The colossal task of re-examining and re-affirming the Buddha's teachings which had been done from time to time since the Buddha passed away, was then accomplished again with tremendous success. Later, the accepted version of Theravada Buddhism was carved on marble tablets and each tablet was housed in a tiered brick structure around the Kuthodaw pagoda at the foot of Mandalay Hill.

Under the king's patronage, Mandalay became a centre of learning and culture; venerable *theras* (monks) with their life-long dedication to the study of the Buddha's teaching, laid down a foundation of Buddhist thought and way of life for all people, regardless of rank, station or education. Closely linked with the spiritual welfare of the people is the upholding of traditions and preservation of ancient arts and crafts. On the whole, King Mindon's dream of national unity is not altogether a lost cause. To this day Mandalay is looked upon as a seat of culture and centre of religious learning.

## SHWEKYIMYIN
## "GOLDEN BIRD SIGHTED"

Most of the Pagodas in Mandalay are just a century old and they hardly have any antiquarian interest; they also lack the ethereal aura and the lyrical quality that only the exuberant imagination of the ancient people could bestow.

Yet there are quite a few pagodas with enchanting backgrounds and one of them is the Shwekyimyin Pagoda. One would hardly associate the present pagoda situated in an active business centre with the picturesque legend the tradition tells to this day. The pagoda is eight centuries older than Mandalay city. The story goes back to the times when the land was young and untamed. Nearby down south, Pagan was already a powerful kingdom ruled by a king named Alaungsithu. His name features in the legends of many pagodas in central Burma.

Alaungsithu was not only a great king and administrator, but also a traveller and explorer of uncommon zeal and courage. The stories of his travels and adventures and wanderings, embellished by incidents with ogres and ogresses, with celestials coming to his aid, are still favourite tales with the young and old.

Alaungsithu had a son named Minshinsaw, a fine prince of a man, well loved by the people, but too quiet and meditative for his royal father's liking. It was on one of his father's trips up the Irrawaddy river that the royal barge stopped on the eastern bank of the place where Mandalay now stands.

*The prince looked on his men, mentally counting them; yes, of course they were only a few, but a happy few brothers; for whoever toiled with him on this untamed land wound be his brother; he did not care what garments the men wore, princely robes or a commoner's garb; such outward things dwelt not in his mind. He would share the honour of striving to realize a dream with anyone who cast his lot with him.*

*"Our story of winning this new land shall the good man tell his son; many men shall think themselves accursed because they were not here, and hold their manhood cheap when we talk of our work and struggle," the prince concluded.*

*The prince's men were greatly moved. "He is full of valour and of kindness, princely in both," they said.*

*The building of Shwekyimyin Pagoda*

*The prince and his men encamped by the river and went inland on exploration trips. It was on the very first day that they saw a beautiful golden bird flying overhead. The bird soared above their heads and flew eastwards and then back to them again, repeating the flight several times. The wise men told the prince that the bird must be leading them to some place. So they followed the bird until they came to the place where today Shwekyimyin Pagoda stands. There the bird stopped his flight and perched on a tree and sang a beautiful note. Then he flew down and at the prince's bidding sat on his shoulder.*

*For some time, the prince and his men played with the bird who ate out of their hands and flew about singing. One of the things the bird did was to fly encircling the spot and landing on the prince's shoulder as if he wanted to tell something. The wise men said that the place must be hallowed ground.*

*The prince and his men made preparations to build a pagoda on the spot and to have his royal father's fare-well gift enshrined therein. All the time, the golden bird kept company and acting as if he understood what the men told him. When the men cried: "Golden Bird, give us a song, we are tired," it would pipe up a cheery tune and the men were gladdened.*

*Cheered by the auspicious omens, the men worked happily. While the foundations of the Pagoda were being laid, another group of men made good use of the brooks and streams to irrigate their fields. Water from the inundated areas were channelled to the reservoirs and landlocked lakes were extended or deepened so that could receive more water in the monsoon.*

*Minshinsaw and his men worked hard, remembering the tradition of King Anawrahta, the prince's ancestor, who with his energy and capable leadership turned the arid plains around Pagan into a land of fields and gardens. Months rolled by and the seasons changed, but the men went on with their work. Even as the beautiful pagoda arose, the lands around blossomed forth in banana plantations, paddy fields, vegetable farms, and mango groves.*

*One important event in the building of the pagoda was the enshrining of the relics in the bejewelled chamber; this was to be followed by the crowning moment, the placing of the* hti, *the iron framework crest on top of the pagoda. These two events must wait till his father's return.*

*The King's Return*

*Preparations were made for the king's return from the North, and the prince's men were agog with excitement. They felt they could match any story of gallantry and achievement the king's men might tell of their travels up the Irrawaddy river. If the explorers in the king's retinue could boast of their daring deeds, they could answer them with the account of their long months of endurance and fortitude, and their battle with the inclemencies of nature.*

*The flotilla of boats came down the river amidst the cheers of welcome by Prince Minshinsaw and his men. As the royal barge approached the landing place, the king would soon be surprised. For, the vast expanse of the river he had seen and left behind was now festooned with sandy islets covered with lush growing fields and plantations. So, this was a visage of the ever-changing moods of the river Irrawaddy.*

*The royal road inland was decorated with bamboo trellis work and rows of luxuriant banana trees laden with bunches of luscious fruits. On either side of the pathway was, as the prince had promised, "a vast tapestry of land spangled with lakes, and interlaced with scintillating canals, running through the varicoloured fields and plantations."*

*When the royal banquet was spread, it meant more surprises for the king. It was not the exotic dishes of fruits, fish, game and vegetables, but the strangely fashioned table-ware in which they were served. Instead of the bejewelled dishes and plates and cups that were used for the king's table, there were exact replicas of remarkable ingenuity.*

*For days, the prince's men had collected banana leaves and let some of them be tinted by the rays of the morning sun, while others were kept fresh and green. They then wove the strips of leaves into several shapes, cups, salvers, dishes and plates so that the sun-tinted ones merged with the green making the things look as if they were worked in gold and emerald. With the sprinkling of coloured blossoms they became the exact copies of the gem-studded dishes of the king's table.*

*The king marvelled at the artistry and patience the men put in to create something so beautiful, and was deeply moved when the prince begged forgiveness for not being able to provide more worthy objects for the occasion.*

*The king declared that the dishes and plates the prince and his men had created were even more precious than gold and bejewelled ones, and that this handicraft must be preserved in honour of the prince's devotion to his father.*

Today, one item in the family celebrations of alms-giving or other festivities, is the set of dishes, cups, goblets and plates fashioned from banana leaves studded with coloured blossoms, the exact replicas of utensils used in the royal court. This handicraft is preserved to this day in Upper Burma towns where culture dies hard.

*The Great Moment*

*It was a great moment when the king and his entourage were led to the pagoda under construction. The inside walls of the relic chamber were studded with gems and one look at the prince, now in the rough woven garb of a peasant, told the king where those gems came from - the prince's regalia.*

*A ghost of a smile hung on the king's lips, as he saws the young prince sun-tanned and more hardy than he had last seen him. The weather-beaten face bore a serene maturity and dignity which none but hard work and tenacity of purpose could give.*

*Overjoyed by his son's achievement, the king poured more jewels and relics into the chamber whose doors were finally closed amidst the triumphant music and songs. But the finest hour was yet to be. It was when the king crowned the pagoda top with the* hti, *the iron framework crest, which was golden, and to which were attached silver bells, whose tintinnabulation concerted with the orchestration of drums and victory songs. The men danced for sheer joy and threw their multicoloured turbans heavenwards, while flying banners joyously rode the breeze.*

*All the time the golden bird, the harbinger of good fortune, took part in the welcome festivities, flying and hopping and singing with delight. The king, told of how the bird guided and inspired the men, declared that the pagoda should be named Shwe-Kyi-Myin ("Golden Bird Sighted").*

## MAHA MYAT MUNI BUDDHA IMAGE: THE ARAKAN PAGODA

The centre of activity in Mandalay is the shrine of Maha Myat Muni Buddha image, or Mahamuni Image as it is usually called , which had been carried from Arakan as a war trophy in 1784. One of the most fervent wishes of a Burmese Buddhist is to have seen the Buddha in person and offered devotions and gifts to him. It is at the shrine of Mahamuni Buddha image that such pious aspiration is - if in a manner - fulfilled, as the legend testifies.

*Once in the land called Dinnyavati, now known as Arakan or Rakhine, a horde of ogres came up from the seas and fed themselves on the people. The devastation was such that it looked as if the human race would be wiped out. It was then that a tribe of Sakkya clansmen from Northern India came, after long years of wandering and searching for new lands. By then Dinnyavati was a scene of death and destruction.*

*True to Sakkya tradition of gallantry and wisdom, the clansmen reorganized the natives to defend their land against the ogres. Under their leadership the ogres were driven away and they set about developing the land and founded a kingdom, Dinnyavati, which soon became a thriving centre of trade, a rendezvous for seamen, overland caravanners and merchants. The dynasty of Sakkya was soon established.*

### *The Great News: The Advent of the Buddha*

It was during the reign of a king named Canda Suriya that the news spread of how Prince Siddattha, of the warrior clan Sakkya, became the Enlightened Buddha. (We should forget, for the moment, that historically King Canda Suriya died around 600 A.D.)

*The news, of course, came in fragments, and at long intervals, often disconnected and incoherent. To many people, it was an interesting conversation piece, something sensational -- a young handsome prince leaving the kingdom and family to take to the woods; his life as an ascetic wearing sack cloth and begging for his daily food; the beautiful wife and son he left behind; later the report of his death through too arduous striving; this last piece was hotly debated; then the news of his being up and about again leading a normal life; this again was also controversial, for how could this prince attain Supreme Light by "taking things easy" when he could not by arduous striving?*

*People talked of nothing else. They waited for caravanners and seamen for the latest development. Each bit of news was passed round and discussed with enthusiasm. The news of Prince Siddattha's attainment of Supreme Light and his Sermon at the Deer Park was the climax. People began to wonder what was in the teaching of Siddattha Gotama Buddha, that made kings and powerful clansmen bow down at his feet. What made young men, noble of lineage, leave their life of luxury and pleasure and follow him to lead a life of poverty and austerity? Why was it that the Buddha's teaching withstood the challenge of the senior teachers of the time?*

### *King Canda Suriya's Enthusiasm*

*Ever since the first news of Gotama Buddha came, King Canda Suriya had been filled with an exultant thrill of awe and wonder. The words, Sakkya Prince, Kappilavatthu City, Migadaya Deer Park, Lumbini Woodlands --- all these struck a chord in his heart; for, had he heard these names and places mentioned by his parents and grand-parents when they told the story of their ancestor's wanderings before they came to Dinnyavati?*

*To think that his own kinsman had become the All Enlightened One and was now teaching the Dhamma, the Law which had never been known or heard in the memory of man, and which could not be challenged by any sage or teacher! As the news of the Buddha developed, the king became more and more excited. He felt that he must have the Buddha come and teach him and his people the Dhamma.*

*However, when the king spoke of his wish to his ministers, they were appalled. After all, the whole thing was a rumour that had been passed round and perhaps, the story had improved with each telling, so there was hardly any point in chasing moonshine.*

*The king was disappointed when he saw that his ministers could not or would not share his enthusiasm. Rarely had he felt more lonely, though he was in the midst of all the pleasure and luxury that life could give.*

*Ministers fell from favour as they could not come up with any helpful suggestion and they dwelt in fear of their life and limb, not daring to say a word; even their silence became an offence. The king became so obsessed with his desire to see the Buddha that he became a sick man losing appetite and sleep. Things came to such a pass that there was a pall of despair in the once pleasurable royal court.*

*One day the king spoke to his favourite consort Omma Devi, who had so long remained silent. He reproved her for being callous and indifferent. Omma Devi, in fact, had been contemplating the matter; she was just biding her time. Now with the king's reproof, she knew the opportune moment had come. She suggested that the king should summon all the sages and wise men of the land and hear what they had to say. Surely someone should come up with a solution.*

### *The Wise Minister's Advice*

*The king immediately proclaimed that all the wise men should assemble at his court. On the day of the assembly, an old minister, who had served the king's father and grandfather and now who had retired from active life, stood up and spoke:*

*"Your Majesty, I have grown old and infirm in the service of your grandfather and your father, and there were affairs of the state, to which but a few had access, and I had the honour of sharing many of the state secrets, one of which was the advent of your birth.*

*"One day, your majesty was barely conceived in the lotus chamber of your mother's womb, when she had a strange dream. She dreamed that her desire to hold the sun and the moon in her hands was fulfilled when your father plucked them out of the heavens and put them in her hands.*

*"Asked to read the dream, I answered that the queen, your mother, would have a son whose wisdom, like the sun, would illuminate the land and whose loving kindness would, like the moon, give happiness and peace to the people. Such was the auspicious event that heralded your coming.*

*"Later when the time ripened, you came forth, like a precious jewel out of a golden casket; that moment a huge satellite came flying from the west and encircled the palace spire and flew westward again. It meant that a great teacher, the All Enlightened One would grace this land with his visit."*

*The old minister's words were like balm to the king's sad heart. He heaped honours and awards on the minister and asked what he should do so that the Buddha would come.*

*Acting on the old minister's advice, the king, his queens and courtiers, took a solemn vow to keep themselves pure in thought, word and deed. Then as each day dawned they assembled in the palace courtyard where offerings of flowers, fruits and candles were arranged, and they recited incantations inviting the Buddha to come and favour them with a visit so that they would be saved from all the evils of suffering. They showered sweet smelling flowers, and gold leaf confetti and grains of multicoloured jewels to welcome the Buddha's coming.*

### *The Buddha received the message*

*All these acts manifested themselves on the mirror of the Buddha's wisdom. The Enlightened One foresaw how his visit to Dinnyavati would lay a foundation for the propagation of his teaching and how it would benefit multitudes of sentient beings for centuries to come. So the Buddha and his disciples journeyed forth to Dinnyavati. The Buddha stood on the hill, and pointing towards Dinnyavati predicted the great future that awaited the territory around the east of the hill. There would arise a prosperous kingdom ruled by the descendants of the Sakkya clan and there his teaching would flourish.*

*Even as the Buddha spoke the words of prophecy, the skies abounded with flying stars, and multitudinous seas arose and swelled in colossal waves. In the city of Dinnyavati the wise men told the king that the Buddha was on the way.*

*So elated by the news were the king and his court that they could no longer stay and wait; they left the city to meet the Buddha on the way.*

### *The King's Welcome Journey*

*The hardships of travelling through the untamed forests and hills, the king hardly felt, so suffused he was with ecstasy. He turned away from appetizing foods his attendants had prepared for him and contented himself with the simple fare of cooked rice and salt.*

*The king's men feared that their royal master might grow weak and sick; but the king was thriving on his spiritual joy and sense of wonder. He was in good health and full of spirits, ever ready to comfort those who were sick or tired or down-hearted. His infectious cheeriness sustained his men throughout the journey.*

*Days later they came upon a plateau. There a great dust storm arose and the king and his men lost their bearings. Frightened by the pall of the darkness surrounding them, they set their hearts on the infinite compassion of the Buddha and prayed for guidance.*

*That moment the irridescent rays of the Buddha's aura in indescribably beautiful colours fell in cascades over the king and his men.*

*Refreshed and overjoyed they soon came upon the Buddha who stretched his hand to welcome them; they all prostrated themselves at the Great One's feet, where they heaped the offerings to express their devotion. All the way back to the city of Dinnyavati the king and men served the Buddha and his disciples like retainers.*

### *The Buddha at Dinnyavati City*

*The people of Dinnyavati city gave a rousing welcome to the Buddha and his disciples who entered the city attended by the king and his courtiers. The Buddha and his disciples were housed in the monastery which had been built for the purpose. Their needs and comforts were adequately attended to by the king and his men.*

*The Buddha taught the king the basic principles of managing the kingdom's affairs with compassion, generosity and tolerance. The officials and commoners alike were given guidance as to how to conduct themselves, so that they could promote happiness and well-being not only in this life but also in the lives to come. The time drew near for the Buddha to end his visit and this was something the king could not face. He simply would not hear of it. His queens and courtiers feared that the Buddha's departure would be the end of the king himself. Something had to be done and done very quickly.*

### *A Compromise*

*By using subtle hints and suggestions, the queens and courtiers finally succeeded in making the king come to terms with the inevitable departure of the Buddha, and he decided to be content with a life-like replica of the Buddha. He begged the Buddha to leave him a likeness so that he and the other devotees could have a replica of the Great One to honour and worship.*

*The Buddha foresaw the infinite good that would result from conceding to such a request, and so he gave his word to comply with the king's wish.*

*The king in his great joy heaped gold and precious stones at the Buddha's feet so that the statue could be cast. It was then that Thagyarmin, king of the celestials, came and at the Buddha's command, transported the treasures to the top of the Siri Makuta Hill on the south west of the city.*

*The Casting of the Image*

*There on the top of the hill Thagyarmin and his retinue saw to the creation of the image, the likeness of the Buddha, to the utmost perfection. The finished image was then enthroned on a bejewelled seat.*

*When the people came to look at the image, they bowed down in deep reverence thinking that it was the Buddha in person. When the Buddha himself came in, they were struck with wonder as if they were seeing two suns arise in the heavens.*

*Even as they gazed in awe, the statue seemed to come to life and a smile lighted on the face as if to greet the great original. Then the Buddha embraced the statue seven times, imparting to it the breath of life. The Buddha exhorted the statue to represent him and his teaching so that multitudes of posterity would benefit. And the rejoicings of the men and gods rose to tumultuous heights. When the Buddha and his disciples left the people of Dinnyavati and their king were well established in the teaching of the Buddha, and the life-like image was there to reinforce their faith and ardour.*

*How the Image was brought to Mandalay*

That was how the Mahamuni Buddha image came into being. How it was brought to Mandalay from Arakan by King Bodawphaya's troops after their campaign in 1784 belongs to history --- authentic and factual.

However, the tedium of historical facts is mercifully enlivened by colourful patches of gossip, rumour and fable. It was the Crown Prince, son and heir of King Bodawphaya, who led the campaign to Arakan and brought back the image to Mandalay.

With so little technical know-how and sophisticated tools and equipment, transporting the image across the Arakan Yoma mountain ranges and later up the river Irrawaddy was indeed no small task. There would be plenty of room for sensational events that could be passed around with more embellishments.

People of Arakan still insist that the Buddha image at Mandalay is not the genuine one, not the one the Buddha himself had embraced seven times and breathed life into. Their story of what happened is as follows:

After the conquest of Arakan the Crown Prince sent one of his generals to go and get the Mahamuni Buddha Image. The general went to the shrine and after offering flowers, candles and fruits and showering confetti to show reverence, requested the image to allow him to carry it to Mandalay.

That moment the great image throbbed as if alive and beads of perspiration fell down in rivulets. The general received the drops in a solid gold goblet and presented it to his master the Crown Prince as an exhibit to support his startling story.

The Crown Prince, however, was determined to get the image. At long last the prince and his men managed to transport the image to the bank of one of those unpredictable, treacherous creeks that meandered through the formidable ranges of Arakan Yoma. The image was then put on the raft which was made for the purpose, but it immediately broke to pieces and the image sank down to the bottom.

The men dived and searched but all their efforts were in vain. The image might as well have been melted and lost forever. So there was only one thing to do --- to cast a replica of the image and carry it to Mandalay. And that was done.

To the Burmese, however, the image now enshrined at Mandalay is the one and only Mahamuni that they know of. To go to Mandalay and pay respects to the Mahamuni Buddha Image means to the Burmese Buddhists, the next best thing to seeing the Buddha himself in person.

The Buddha embraced the image seven times to give it life.

## TAUNGPYONE
## "WISH-FULFILLING PAGODA"

Taungpyone, a village 9 miles north of Mandalay is well known for the annual ritual feast held in July-August, an occasion for unrestrained merry- making, drinking and dancing, where people just let themselves go. In the middle of the village is a hillock with a pagoda on top. It is a cave temple after the style of pagodas in Pagan. Not far from the pagoda is a *nat*-shrine, a shrine for local deities Min Gyi and Min Lay, in whose honour the annual feast is held.

The story of Min Gyi and Min Lay is closely associated not only with the "Wish-fulfilling pagoda", but also with faraway places like Thaton, an ancient Mon city down south on the Tenessarim coast, Mount Popa, and Pagan, the capital of the first Burmese kingdom. Taungpyone Pagoda was built by King Anawrahta of Pagan (ruled 1044-1077 A.D.), the builder of the first Burmese kingdom and also a religious and social reformer who firmly established Theravada Buddhism in the land.

A colourful patchwork of romantic stories is woven around Anawrahta and his hero-knights whose physical prowess - some of them had the strength of five elephants - and exploits in the battlefield and romantic adventures shimmered through the sombre pages of history. Their names live today not only in folk-lore but also in songs, drama, films, and above all, in the hearts of the people. To tell the story of Taungpyone, and the local deities Min Gyi and Min Lay, we must start with a flash-back to Thaton, the ancient Mon City down south by the sea, and King Anawrahta's campaigns to obtain the Buddhist Scriptures, an essential element for the establishment of Buddhism in Pagan.

### *Two Dark Strangers at Thaton*

*The story begins with the brothers Byatwi and Byatta, the two dark strangers from India, who were shipwrecked off the Tenessarim coast and picked up by a venerable monk and taken to his monastery. There they lived and earned their keep by attending to the needs of the monk.*

*One day the monk took the two brothers into the forest to collect fruits and faggots. Wandering around, they came upon something strange under a tree. At first, it looked like the body of a baby, but it had a beautiful golden colour and it smelled like a bunch of luscious bananas.*

*The venerable monk at once knew what it was: a left-over shell of a man who had changed himself into a* zawgyi *or demi-god. The monk explained to the brothers that a man who wished to be a zawgyi took to the woods and practised austerities and contemplation; he also collected herbs that had magic qualities and crushed them on a stone slab chanting appropriate mantras. The triumphant moment came when he had taken the right amount of herbs at the auspicious time; he then took a new form, a demi-god in red flaming robes, endowed with super-normal powers, like flying into the air, slipping into the dark bowels of the earth, and travelling under water like an amphibian; above all, he would have longivity that could only be measured in thousands. Of his old body, only small remains were left, and it was what the monk and the two brothers found in the woods. The monk knew that whoever ate up the remains would be endowed with some super-normal powers, though not as much as the* zawgyi *himself, but enough to be a super-man of great strength and possessing immunity against death-dealing weapons. So he told the brothers to carry the remains to the monastery, intending to eat it in good time.*

*It so happened that the venerable monk never managed to have his fabulous snack, because he fell asleep tired from the journey; while he was asleep, the two brothers, unable to resist the appetizing aroma, ate the whole thing between them.*

*The two brothers suddenly found*

*themselves in possession of super-normal powers. When they jumped, they rose high up into the air; when they leaned on a tree it fell down like a stick. When they tried lifting the monastery building, it came away in their hands like a plaything. They then decided to play a trick; they lifted the monastery building with the sleeping monk inside and transported it into a dark corner of the forest. When the monk woke up he thought he was in a terrible nightmare, especially when the brothers lifted the building again and returned it to the old place. The venerable monk realized what had happened but he could do nothing. He had only to put up with the brothers' mischievous tricks.*

*The Brothers became bandits*

*Later, things went out of hand when avaricious self-seeking people flattered the brothers into becoming bandits. They had a large following and the band of Byatwi and Byatta became the terror of the land. They scourged the country and people lived in fear of their life and limb.*

*King Manuha, ruler of Thaton, set a high reward on the heads of the brothers, but, what with their extraordinary powers, they could not be seized until one day one of the commanders hit upon a plan. Perhaps he could get hold of Byatwi the elder brother, if not both. Byatwi had a mistress in the city, a girl named Ma Oh Zar, whom he visited at night. The commander was told by wise men that Byatwi's super-normal powers could be destroyed by defilement, that is by making him walk where women's nether garments were hung overhead. That was quite easy, since the commander had been informed of Byatwi's movements at night. The commander's men secretly did what was necessary where Byatwi was wont to pass. That night, as soon as Byatwi passed the spot, he was seized with a horrible spasm of itching. He at once knew that something evil was afoot. The next moment the men were upon him. When he tried to leap as of old, he found that he could no longer rise out of the reach of his captors.*

*Byatwi would not die*

*However, it was not the end of Byatwi. When the men tied him to the stake and tried to beat him with clubs, hack him with swords, and stab him with spears, they could not so much as give him a scratch. Even though his super-normal powers were gone there was something that would not give way: his undaunted spirit.*

*Until and unless Byatwi voluntarily gave up his life he would not die, even though he suffered pain. He bore the pain knowing full well that his tormenters would have to give up; it was the battle of the wills. The commander had to think of a ruse. He taunted Byatwi, saying how foolish he was to suffer pain when he had nothing to live for, his mistress Ma Oh Zar having betrayed him for the reward. With the ample dowry she had, she could choose any nobleman in King Manuha's court. Byatwi did not believe the story. Then the commander told Byatwi that he could produce proof; his mistress Ma Oh Zar herself would tell Byatwi that she wanted him to die - this she would do by a gesture. Ma Oh Zar would come to Byatwi with a quid of betel and a cup of water, which, the commander explained, was, according to the local custom, a gift to a dying man.*

*Byatwi, being a foreigner, did not know that the 'custom' was invented by the commander on the spur of the moment to suit his purpose. The commander said that if Ma Oh Zar did indicate a wish that Byatwi should live, he would let him go free. But if, on the other hand, Ma Oh Zar should bring a quid of betel and a cup of water, then he should be man enough to read the message and meet his death.*

*Then the commander told Ma Oh Zar a different story. He said that Byatwi had been pardoned by the king and that he was waiting for her. The woman, overjoyed by the news, was about to rush to her lover. The commander, as if in an afterthought, said: was she going to him empty-handed? Why, she might take him a quid of betel and a cup of water. And Ma Oh Zar did.*

*When Byatwi saw Ma Oh Zar coming towards him with the ominous gift, he was completely overcome; his loved one's betrayal stronger than the executioners' swords quite vanquished him and his mighty heart burst. He scarcely heard his mistress's protestations of love nor did he feel her tender arms around him.*

*Now that Byatwi was dead, the wise man suggested to the king to make good use of his remains for the defence of the city. Byatwi's flesh and insides were buried at the four corners of the city walls, which were then sprinkled with his blood. In this way, Byatwi's spirit would have to guard the city against invaders.*

*Meanwhile, Byatwi's brother Byatta had escaped to Pagan and had taken asylum at Anawrahta's court. He became a trusted henchman of the king and his assignment was to train the king's men in horsemanship and other martial arts. His headquarters was the area around Mount Popa. Since his real commission was a guarded royal secret, he was only known as the supplier of rare flowers to the queens and ladies of the court. It was at Popa that Byatta met his love, Mai Wunna, a forest nymph who lived on flowers. When their two sons were born, the king honoured them by giving a solid gold pot to each; they were known as Shwe Phyin Gyi and Shwe Phyin Lay, "Gold Pot the Elder" and "Gold Pot the Younger". Later they were called Min Gyi and Min Lay, "the Elder Lord" and "the Younger Lord".* *

*King Anawrahta and Thaton*

Anawrahta was interested in Thaton, not so much as a potential for military conquest but as a future alliance in cultural and religious works which were part of his plan for the unification of the Burmese kingdom.

It was not only swash-buckling heroes that Anawrahta had around him but also sagacious statesmen like Kyansittha, later his successor,and Shin Arahan, a learned monk, his spiritual advisor. Shin Arahan had explicitly told Anawrahta that in order to introduce Theravada Buddhism into the land, he must have authentic writings of Buddhist Scriptures and learned monks to teach them. At that time Thaton was the centre of Buddhist learning in Burma. It was essential that Anawrahta seek the help of King Manuha to get the Scriptures and the learned monks from Thaton.

Anawrahta duly sent a mission to Thaton requesting King Manuha send him the Scriptures and some of the learned teachers to Pagan, so that Theravada Buddhism would be well propagated throughout the land. In those days, geographical distance and lack of proper communications bred misunderstanding. To King Manuha of Thaton, the men of central Burma were but warring tribes, not worthy of the Buddha's teaching; and he said so in no uncertain terms to the men of Anawrahta's mission.

*Campaign against Thaton*

*War became inevitable and Anawrahta's forces marched to Thaton and laid siege to the city. But they were up against the super-normal powers of Byatwi's spirit who guarded the city walls. Anawrahta's men could not come within a stone's throw of the city walls. Anawrahta sent Byatta, who knew the terrain well, to gather information regarding the city's defences. One night, Byatta left his attendants behind and approached the city walls from which his men were repulsed by some mysterious forces. They had come back from their offensive operations with attacks of hysteria and stories of headless monsters and other creations of the heat-oppressed brain. Byatta suspected something evil and he had to find out what it was.*

* In central Burma areas the Burmese expression for 'pot' is *Phyin,* which in the manner of mono-syllabic languages is synonymous with 'inferior'; hence the names Shwe Phyin Gyi and Shwe Phyin Lay are often interpreted as inferior gold.

People still use the expression "to ask for a quid of betel and a cup of water" in everyday conversation when they are in a desperate situation in which all hope is lost. One wonders if the unwillingness of the Burmese to walk under the clothesline on which women's nether garments are hung had its source in Byatwi's tragic experience.

*Byatta was looking hard at the city wall as if commanding it to give up its secret when he was startled by some mysterious presence. He suddenly found himself gazing at a wraith-like apparition, shadowy but recognizable as his late brother Byatwi. Byatta shuddered, unwonted goose-pimples arose all over his body. In the well-remembered voice of his brother, the spirit of Byatwi told him that he could not but guard the city walls as commanded by King Manuha. He had been completely enthralled as his body had been used to guard the city walls. Byatta insisted that there might be a chance of Anawrahta's forces penetrating the city walls; could Byatwi help? Byatwi replied that the weakest point in the city's defences was a space not covered by his blood, for he would be powerless over that area, though it was but "a sitting hen's gap in the wall".*

Once the secret was in the hands of Anawrahta's men, the city fell. Buddhist Scriptures, learned monks and the royal family of King Manuha were brought back to Pagan and Theravada Buddhism became firmly established in the land of Tampadipa, as Anawrahta's kingdom was called.

Today, close by the ruined remains of the southern wall of the city of Thaton is a small brook running into the city. Local people point out to visitors that it is the "sitting hen's gap in the wall" where Anawrahta's forces made their assault. Right on the place are sculptured likenesses of Byatwi, and Byatta who died during the siege, and Ma Oh Zar, Byatwi's mistress, whose spirit had been reconciled to that of her lover.

*Back to Mandalay:*

*the building of "Wish-fulfilling Pagoda"*

Now that Byatta had given his life during the Thaton campaign, Anawrahta took his two sons Min Gyi and Min Lay into his service. They were stationed at Taungpyone near Mandalay to see to the Building of a pagoda wherein the emerald Buddha image, a trophy from a campaign to Yunan, was to be enshrined.

Min Gyi and Min Lay had distinguished themselves during the Yunan campaign, and the fantastic stories of their exploits were the talk of the town. The two brothers had proved themselves to be worthy sons of Byatta who was nothing less than a super-man in the eyes of the people.

So that the people of all levels could participate in the building of the pagoda, the king had decreed that each person must bring a brick to the building site. Attracted by the glamour of the gallant heroes, Min Gyi and Min Lay, and inspired by the honour of having a pagoda to grace the locality, the people rallied round with heart and soul. It was a happy time for all people coming to the site in groups, each carrying a brick, accompanied by music troupes, dances and songs. Everyone had a sense of belonging to the pagoda and the news that the king himself would be favouring the place with a visit when the pagoda was completed delighted them all the more.

The pagoda under construction became something special to each and everyone and each felt his or her own wish would be fulfilled. So fervent was their faith that the wish of each person was fulfilled in some way. So the pagoda came to be called "Wish-fulfilling pagoda".

*Yet there was an ominous shadow of fear amidst the festivities - it was the dominant power of the brothers Min Gyi and Min Lay who ruled the place. Endowed with good looks, gallant and dashing, they were courted and flattered by hangers-on who led them into corruption. Min Gyi, the elder brother, who was the quieter of the pair, often tried to play mentor to his younger brother albeit with something less than success. Stories of Min Lay's drinking bouts and licentiousness were whispered around. Respectable people tried to avoid them and folk locked up their daughters when they heard that Min Lay was around.*

### *Ma Shwe Oo, a maiden chaste and pure*

*One of the most irksome of Min Gyi's responsiblilities was to keep his brother from amorous adventures which were becoming increasingly vicious. Thus when Min Lay set himself upon winning a girl named Ma Shwe Oo, Min Gyi feared the worst. Min Gyi knew only too well that she was not just another girl to be trifled with. First, she was virtuous and pure, not at all like the blithe and buxom maids Min Lay was used to. Second, she was the daughter of the headman and administrator of Inkyinyaw village, a man respected and loved by the people.*

*If Min Lay thought for a moment that he could satisfy a whim and ride away in triumph, he was greatly mistaken. He was politely but firmly put off, because Ma Shwe Oo already had a lover, who had been accepted by her parents.*

*In a society that considered seduction of a woman married, or promised to another, as a crime worse than murder, Min Lay, notwithstanding his popularity, glamour and power, would not be able to get away with it. Min Gyi tried to warn and reason, but his brother would not listen. Ma Shwe Oo's modesty had stirred Min Lay more strongly than any strumpet with all her vigour. Min Lay visited Ma Shwe Oo's home, planted himself at the loom where the girl worked, and pressed his suit.*

*At first, Ma Shwe Oo put him off, gently explaining that she was already affianced to Ko Yin Maung, a forester who was then away on a logging expedition up north, and that it was unseemly for Min Lay to harbour such a thought. When Min Lay became more and more vehement in his wooing, Ma Shwe Oo could no longer be courteous. She hurled abuses at him: she called him a homeless wanderer, rootless, not belonging to any respectable clan, a man without a country, the progeny of the trash of a man who was washed ashore from nowhere; an alien of unknown breed; a mongrel; and just because the king had favoured him with honours - honours which sat on him as a giant's robe on a miserable dwarf - he was giving himself airs; a man who was not worthy of touching the hem of her skirt, and so on and so forth.*

*Min Lay in all his young errant life had never had such a dressing down. Used to having his own way, Min Lay for a moment wanted to kill this slip of a girl. But then, it would not do for the great lover to kill a girl who refused him. He would be the laughing-stock. He must change his tactics.*

*Min Lay acted as if he did not hear a word of Ma Shwe Oo's words. He laughed, cajoled and teased the girl, playing the buffoon. He fell at her feet declaring that he would die then and there for the love of her, until Ma Shwe Oo ran out of her colourful expletives.*

### *Ma Shwe Oo took flight*

*As the situation worsened, Ma Shwe Oo's parents, helped by loyal friends, took flight and tried to lie low in a village called Ye-gyi where the parents of Ko Yin Maung, Ma Shwe Oo's intended lived. The family lost no time in having the marriage of Ko Yin Maung and Ma Shwe Oo contracted. Then the parents made arrangements to report the matter to the king, who would arrive soon to witness the completion of the "Wish-fulfilling Pagoda". Once the matter was known to the king, they would be safe. Ma Shwe Oo and her family were helped and supported by other families whose daughters had been unwilling victims of Min Lay's debaucheries. They all prepared cases to be reported to the king.*

Min Lay woos but Ma Shwe Oo scorns.

*All the time, Min Lay looked for Ma Shwe Oo who seemed to have disappeared altogether. He became more and more enraged, as his hangers-on were unable to pry into the secret of the girl's hiding place, which was loyally guarded by their friends. He threw himself into drinking bouts so completely that he became careless and negligent of his duties.*

*Meanwhile, the building of the pagoda went on, each person bringing a brick to the site.*

*King Anawrahta at Taungpyone*

*Finally, the day came for the king to visit the pagoda. Inside the temple were local officials to welcome the king and his entourage. Outside the temple was a huge cheering crowd eager to get a glimpse of the king and his court who had honoured them with the visit.*

*There was a tumult of cheering as the king made his appearance and the people fell on their knees to pay homage. The king and his courtiers entered the temple and looked around to see if everything were perfect. All of a sudden a fearful hush fell on the crowd; each looked at the other in consternation. They then followed the king's gaze up the wall of the shrine. There were two spaces left unattended for two bricks. Who had dared to fail in the duty of bringing the bricks? Everyone knew that it was Min Gyi and Min Lay who had failed the site.*

*Even before anyone could utter a word, the king's men came in with the request that the headman of Inywa village and his family sought royal audience.*

*With the king's permission, Ma Shwe Oo, her parents and her husband Ko Yin Maung were brought into the king's presence. Ma Shwe Oo's father pointed to the space of the missing bricks and said that the two brothers Min Gyi and Min Lay were responsible for the omission. This was a serious crime in itself. But there were other charges against Min Lay, carefully prepared and supported by families who were dishonoured by Min Lay's misadventures. The king ordered the brothers to be executed, which was duly done.*

*The Brothers' Spirits beg a favour from the king*

*On the day the king was to leave for Pagan, the royal barge would not move from its moorings; it stayed stuck as if held by an unseen hand. The king suspected evil and at once struck the water with his sword. And there on the surface of the river appeared the two brothers Min Gyi and Min Lay; they were kneeling, with their hands clasped in supplication.*

*Commanded by the king to say what they wished, the brothers asked the king's forgiveness for their negligence of duty, but in consideration of their former services, would the king be so gracious as to grant them a place to live. The king, moved by the brothers' plight, decreed that the Taungpyone area should be theirs; they would be the vassal lords with all the feudal privileges of tithes and taxes.*

Friends and followers of the brothers built shrines for them and held annual feasts in their honour, a tradition that lives on to this day.

*Death could not end Min Lay's love*

Even though Min Lay had passed a way to the existence of a spirit, his love for Ma Shwe Oo did not die. He was still determined to win her. He could manifest himself to her and say words of love. He said that he had died for love of her, and would die a thousand deaths before he stopped loving her.

*Ko Yin Maung had made ready for another logging expedition, even though his young wife was loath to let him go on such a long and dangerous journey. But then, he had to provide for their future. When Ko Yin Maung left, Ma Shwe Oo busied herself at the loom. Her small home industry was not only for domestic use but for the market. She was well known for her skill and artistry and Ko Yin Maung was a lucky man, especially in those days when a woman who could not weave was considered no better than a cripple. Ma Shwe Oo, working on her loom, counted on her fingers and waited for the day of Ko Yin Maung's return. She said to herself happily that she no longer had to fear the unwelcome attentions of Min Lay - but this she said too soon.*

*Suddenly, there floated in the air a fetid smell of blood and green leaves and Ma Shwe Oo quaked with an unknown dread, breaking out in goose-flesh. She felt some evil presence nearby. Even though she guessed who it was, she was frightened even to think of that name. When she finally found enough courage to look she saw Min Lay in person. He was dressed as usual in gorgeous robes with a flaming red scarf tied round his chest; he held his sword in hand as if ready for action; the bejewelled scabbard hung on his waist band. He showed the same audacious face with the same lascivious leer which Ma Shwe Oo hated so much. Yet there was something different; and Ma Shwe Oo shuddered at the sight of it. For, at Min Lay's feet crouched a huge tiger ferociously growling and baring his teeth. It was Min Lay's trusted servant ready to pounce on anyone at his master's bidding.*

*Ma Shwe Oo was struck dumb when Min Lay spoke. He said he had died for love of her, and she should at least be kind to him; could he not be her spirit lover coming to her sometimes and talking to her? He could watch her pretty hands work at the loom; as they were no longer in the same plane of existence, why should she not be kind to him? And the most important of all, could she not say that she was sorry that he had to die that way and that she cared for him just a little?*

*Ma Shwe Oo was outraged; she said that any feeling she could spare for him except that of hatred and contempt would be a betrayal to her adored husband Ko Yin Maung, whose feet he did not deserve to touch; to think that such an accursed thing like him who had died like a baited animal at the stake - a beastly death for one so beastly - should dare to come near her and speak like that!.*

*Min Lay taunted Ma Shwe Oo saying what a wonder that she preferred that milk-sop of a husband who would not dare to come anywhere near his sword point, a man who instead of keeping his wife in style, as she deserved, kept her at the loom working her fingers to the bone. Min Lay could shower her with silks and jewels and she would not have to sit at the loom, but live like a queen. When Ma Shwe Oo was not at all moved by his words, Min Lay threatened to set the tiger on her. Even as the tiger snarled and growled Ma Shwe Oo said he could do his worst. Min Lay did not wish to hurt her, so he commanded the tiger to seize her girdle and carry her out of the village.*

*There was a hue and cry in the village. Min Lay made himself invisible except to Ma Shwe Oo and the people thought that it was just an ordinary tiger. They gave chase to the "spirit tiger" which soon disappeared among the trees. Min Lay followed the tiger into the woods, all the time pressing Ma Shwe Oo to say just a few words of love and give him permission to visit her sometimes. Ma Shwe Oo remained adamant. She would rather die in the fangs of the tiger than submit to such unwarranted violence.*

The trail of the tiger carrying Ma Shwe Oo runs through the fields on the south of Taungpyone, and it is today marked by places bearing names that tell the story of the girl's macabre journey. Each place is marked by a shrine or a pagoda. On the spot where Ma Shwe Oo's girdle gave way and dropped to the ground is a shrine; it bears the name Khar-si-kya, which means "where the girdle dropped". An old broken down pagoda marks the place where the girl bled to death and it is called Thway-set-kya ("Blood drops fell").

The place where Ma Shwe Oo's flowers fell is marked by a grove of Tharapi flowering trees (Calophyllum Spp.). It is a sanctified place; when the blossoms come forth in April, no one would pluck them for the market or personal use; instead, people celebrate a flower-picking festival where the flowers are gathered and offered at the shrine of Ma Shwe Oo's spirit.

Virtuous to the end, Ma Shwe Oo suffered the fangs of the spirit tiger rather than submit to Min Lay. The trail where the tiger dragged her through the fields can still be found today south of Taungpyone, Mandalay.

The shrine for Ma Shwe Oo's spirit is on what is known as Thakin-ma Taung ("Milady's hill") named in her honour. She is known in the area as Thakin-ma. She is very much respected and loved by the people. There is also a shrine on Mandalay Hill with her image in it. On Thakin-ma Taung, a grand palace of a shrine had been built with images of herself and her husband Ko Yin Maung, who died of a broken heart and joined her there. An annual festival is held in her honour at the end of August.

The story of Ma Shwe Oo lives today in songs, plays and in films. In the In-Kyin village, Ma Shwe Oo's birthplace, the place where her family had lived is marked by a huge stone boulder. It was said to be the stone Min Lay carried from the nearby hill to show his strength when he was courting her. The place, up to this day, is not used for residence, as people believe that bad luck would attend whoever lived there.

At *nat-pwe* or Ritual Feasts which are held today all over the country and in the heart of Rangoon, people watch with awe and wonder as the professional mediums are possessed, one after another, by the pantheon of *nats* and spirits and as the mediums perform traditional dances. One of the highlights on the third and last day is the performance of the man who is possessed by Min Lay's Tiger-Spirit. He would make a leap like a feline animal, crawl and crouch and clutch a coconut, scratch and break open its cover and husks with his claws and his fangs, to the amazement of the spectators.

## SHWEKYETYET PAGODA

There is yet one place to see before leaving Mandalay, the Shwekyetyet Pagoda.

The traveller turns west out of Mandalay and passes through Amarapura which had been the royal seat since 1783 till King Mindon moved the capital to Mandalay in 1857. There is an interesting footnote to history connected with the abandoning of Amarapura as capital:

*King Mindon wished to know how people felt about moving the royal city to Mandalay, so he sent his brother, the Crown Prince to go disguised as a commoner among people and take note of what they said. The road between Amarapura, the old city and the new city that was being built was a hub-bub of activity; a long caravan of bullock carts carrying building materials creaked endlessly along.*

*The disguised Prince asked for a lift in one of the carts and he fell into conversation with the old man who was driving. In a round-about way the Prince brought up the topic of moving the royal seat to Mandalay and asked how the old man felt about it.*

*The old cart driver thought the whole thing totally unnecessary; after all, what was wrong with Amarapura? Why all this fuss and trouble? The Prince asked if the old man thought things might be better, when the younger brother came to the throne.*

*Here, the old man grimaced and said: "No bastard from that blank --- blank - blankety --- family would be any better!" Back at the palace the royal brothers had a good laugh over the outspoken answer; they appreciated a good joke even when it went against them. It was not every day that royalty was so entertained.*

*The story was passed around not only in the court circles, but also among the commoners. The spontaneous remark seemed to fit not only 'high dames and mighty earls', but also 'lowly churls'. It remains to this day a favourite expression to describe just about anybody's kith and kin (sometimes, even your own), who invariably qualifies for the epithet. No amount of repetition throughout the century has tarnished the brilliance of its biting wit.*

Shwekyetyet Pagoda.

Leaving Amarapura, the traveller goes on towards the bridgehead of Ava Bridge. But just before he or she gets there, there is, on the right side, a small pathway winding and losing itself into the woods. It has a sign board which reads: "To Shwekyetyet Pagoda". A dirt road leads to a small hill.

The climb up the hill is easy and pleasant; a few white pagodas crawl up from half way to the top and tower above the sandy beach, which is alive with fishing boats and washing women and children playing paddly pools.

Far away on the other side of the river looms the long wooded Sagaing range, dark and moody, but for the pagodas, some golden, others gleaming white, each riding on the crest of rolling hills - a scene once described: "Like white sails on the Atlantic". The wide brimming river mirrors the reflection of the Sagaing ridge and lengthens it toward the rock cliff on which Shwekyetyet pagoda stands.

The pagoda is named after the rock cliff: it is called Shwe-kyet-yet ("Golden Fowl's Run") because according to the legend, the place was once the habitat of the Buddha-to-be, who in one of his former lives was born a Golden Fowl.

*The Golden Fowl was menaced by hunters who were under orders of the king to catch him; so he and his brother, after days of evading the trappers, found safety on this rock cliff. The elder brother Golden Fowl roosted on the top and his younger brother a little way down the slope, as marked by the two groups of pagodas.*

Later, yarns of the ancient legend were woven into authentic historical events. In the 3rd century B.C., when Emperor Asoka sent out Buddhist missionaries to distant lands, a team of *thera* (monks) came to Burma, then called Sunarparanta. One of the *thera,* having supernormal powers, saw that the rock-cliff was indeed the habitat of the Buddha-to-be, then born a Golden Fowl.

So, with the help of the tribes and chieftains, they built a stupa and enshrined the Buddha's relics therein. In 1165, when the first Burmese kingdom flourished in Pagan, King Narapatisithu repaired the shrine and he did something rather unusual. He put heavy guards around the cliff; and no one could come near the place but on pain of death. Why he did it is told in the legend:

*Narapatisithu was only a younger brother of the then reigning king. One day, foresters came to the Queen Mother and presented her with a young maid, who they said was born out of a bamboo stem. (Such was the immaculate manner in which the fairy-girl characters in legends were born).*

*She was named Veluvati, Bamboo Maid, a gentle ethereal creature she was; but her ear lobes were such that they detracted from the perfection of her beauty. The Queen Mother presented her to the elder son the king, but he was not very enthusiastic about making her his queen.*

*So Veluvati was given to the younger son Narapatisithu. Later the Queen Mother had some surgery performed on the girl's ear lobes, the only flaw in the otherwise enchanting face. One day while the king was holding court he saw Veluvati, bedecked with jewels as befitted a Crown Princess modestly sitting by her proud adoring husband. The king was filled with an unseemly desire for her. To think that he had let this treasure of a maiden slip through his hands! He was determined to have her by fair means or foul; and unfortunately, foul it had to be. The king sent for his brother and ordered him to march to the border where, he said, there was an uprising to be quelled.*

*The prince was not without misgivings. He bade a sad farewell to his wife and left instructions with his faithful servant Maung Pyi to jump on the prince's own fleet-footed white horse and follow him post haste should anything untoward happen.*

A beautiful maid, born out of the hollow of the bamboo, and her royal lover.

*As soon as the prince departed, the king took Veluvati by force. The faithful servant Muang Pyi did the only thing possible - threw himself on the white horse and rode hard to his master. Riding through the dark night in the woods, Muang Pyi lost his bearings. He found himself encircling a hill many times. At last he reached the bank of a stream. To his anxious and weary eyes the stream was overflowing with surging waves and he laid himself down in despair to await the light of dawn. It so happened that the prince was encamped on the other side of the stream. The horse, scenting the presence of his master, neighed all night. Muang Pyi, worn out with exhaustion, fell fast asleep.*

*The prince having found out that there was no uprising on the border, lay on his bed tormented by the worst fears of the king's intentions, when he heard the neighing of his trusty horse. Early in the morning, Muang Pyi saw to his terror and astonishment, that the stream was dry. He crossed it and reached his master and reported the matter. When the prince learned that Muang Pyi had spent the night on the other side of the stream, when every moment counted, he was beside himself with rage. He ordered Muang Pyi to be executed on the spot.*

*The prince then marched to the city of Pagan. On the way he stopped at the rock cliff where Shwekyetyet pagoda stands today. He entered the shrine and made a wish that he might be successful in his plot against the king.*

*Having nothing to make an offering to the Buddha image, he took off the robe he was wearing and stretched his hand to put it respectfully on the shoulder of the Buddha statue. That instant, he saw something his normal senses would never have though possible. The statue suddenly became alive and its shoulders moved even so slightly to receive the gift.*

*The prince and his men were heartened and Narapatisithu became sure that good gods were on their side. After all who would want an adulterous and incestuous king on the throne? The coup was successful and Narapatisithu became king. Now the king, realizing how effectively the shrine on the "Golden Fowl's Run" had fulfilled his own prayer, put guards on the place. He did not want any of his enemies to find their way there.*

The story of Shwekyetyet pagoda is associated with one of the best quoted pieces of Burmese literature, four short verses written by a wise minister of that time, Ananda-thuriya. He was one of the victims of King Narapatisithu's fury over the loss of his queen to another man - a situation the Burmese idiom describes as "being possessed by Deindalein *Nat*", which might be rendered as "a cuckold husband's fury".

The king committed many cruel and thoughtless crimes; he ordered the wise minister to be executed for no other reason than that he had not been able to dissuade the king from his adulterous act.

The four verses submitted by the minister so moved the king that he ordered a reprieve, only to be confronted by his officials who supplicated before him with the words: "Mercy on us, O Great King, the sword of power had gone and done its duty!"

The spirit of non-vengeance in the poem, however, had a lasting effect on the king. He could not but see himself a baser being, who had perpetrated acts of senseless cruelty, making innocent ones bear the brunt of his mad fury.

*The weight of his wrongs - starting with the killing of his faithful servant Muang Pyi - lay heavy on him. His tortured mind turned to the shrine on the Golden Fowl's Run Hill. Why had the powers that be granted his wish, if it meant such evil consequences?*

*The king then sought the counsel of the venerable* thera *(monks). They told him that it was not the powers above that had granted his wish; his wish had been fulfilled by virtue of his own deed; he had paid respects at the shrine and*

Riding hard the whole night, the faithful servant fell asleep, not realizing that his master whom he sought was close by.

*made the offering of his own robe spontaneously; the force of the deed was a neutral thing; if he had used it to his own evil purpose, it was his own responsibility. The venerable thera then advised the king not to brood ever the past, which would be no help at all, but to be aware of the evil nature of his past actions and be mindful in future. His own realization and mindfulness alone would help him to lead a good life, and to be at peace with himself.*

*The king realized his own evil deeds and he had to steel himself to be man enough to admit that he alone was responsible for them. He took the first step toward a better life by passing an edict that all sentences of extreme penalty must be stayed a month until the king had reviewed them.*

He no longer wanted the "sword of power to go and do its duty" at the slightest provocation.

In memory of his faithful servant Muang Pyi, who appeared before him as a spirit, the king granted him the area around his place of execution as his domain. The local inhabitants gave an annual feast to the "Lord of the White Horse", as Muang Pyi has come to be know to this day. He was, or rather is, one of the genial good spirits of the pantheon. He is represented as riding a white horse.

The king also commemorated Muang Pyi's last fateful ride giving appropriate names to places, so that his story might be remembered. The hill which Muang Pyi encircled many times is today known as Myin-hle-taung ("Horse-encircling Hill"); Kut-taw-yar ("Place of Execution") is the name of the place where Muang Pyi met his fate; the island on which Muang Pyi's body lay after floating down the river is Shwe-pyi-kyun (" the Island of Golden Muang Pyi"). "Golden" is an affectionate suffix the king gave him, a faithful servant who gave his life for his master.

As for the wise minister Ananda–thuriya, he needs no memorial; his four verses live on to this day, outliving all the monuments, marble or gilded:

1. If one person,
   To upward rises,
   Down goes the other,
   Accordingly,
   Such is the law,
   Of nature.

2. In gilded home,
   He dwells in state,
   With lords and peers,
   Happiness he enjoys.
   Like a bubble,
   That rises up
   On the sea's surface
   Lasts but a lifetime.

3. With compassion,
   Spared I might be,
   From death, and yet,
   This end so certain,
   Must all men face,
   This solid flesh
   Being so mortal,
   The fate of all beings.

4. I bow down to thee,
   My Leige-lord king,
   With deep respect,
   I, thy faithful slave.
   On our way through
   This cycle of rebirth,
   If we shall meet,
   Desire not I,
   Any vengeance.
   With love deep and true,
   I'd let thee be,
   No grudge I bear;
   Only forgiveness.
   For, it's in mine
   Own blood dwells
   The destroyer,
   Impermanance,
   Leading to the end,
   Inevitable.

Before the traveller leaves Shwekyetyet hill, he wonders if he should make a wish at the shrine. The risk of having his wish fulfilled is so great that he is not sure if he is prepared to play such high stakes..........

CHAPTER VII

# SAGAING: RETREAT AMONG THE HILLS

When a native of Mandalay feels he is in need of a change from the grindstone of daily labour, he or she says, "I think I'll go West". That is to say that one is going into retreat among the Sagaing Hills on the west bank of the river Irrawaddy.

"Going-West" that way promises a rare spell of rest and repose among the shrines and monasteries, far from the crowd's ignoble strife. Even as the pilgrim crosses the Ava bridge, he sees the hilltops, each crested with a pagoda, the banners proclaiming the Buddha's teaching, the refuge from all ills and tribulations that human life is heir to. Towering above all is the golden Ponnyashin Pagoda, where tourists and devout pilgrims alike go first.

The hilltop on which the pagoda stands can be reached by motor road, but the pilgrim whose sweet and wholesome hours are reckoned with the tinkling of temple bells, is not pressed for time; this pilgrim prefers to ascend one of the brick stair ways zig-zagging up the hill. There are four stairways up the hill, each from a different direction. The tiered roofs protect the pilgrim from sun and rain. The way usually taken is the one with a lone crested lion figure sitting at the foot of the stairs.

This locality is called Thayetpinseik, literally "Mango tree port", a terminal for horse-carts, cars, buses, and boats plying the river. There is not a single mango tree in sight; whence the mango tree name, no one knows. Nor can anyone explain why there is only one single crested Lion, when it is customary to have a pair.

The unexplained is all part of the fantasy that is the Sagaing Hill. Today, the place is the abode of monks, nuns and ascetics, and it is also an occasional retreat for devotees in need of rest from the stress of life.

In the days beyond the memory of man, hermits and ascetics dwelt in the primeval forests. As the pilgrim goes up the hill, he or she looks at the gnarled, knotted trees, their serpentine roots clawing at the rocks and boulders. They look like the fossils of some ancient mythical monsters, fire-breathing dragons, ogres, gnomes and demons. The delicate scent of the white blossoms refreshes the pilgrims, whose thoughts dwell on the loving kindness of the hermits of those times, who lived in peace not only with wild beasts but also with the mythical monsters.

## LUNZEDI

The pilgrim takes a brief rest at one of those places, a small platform with seats and kiosks of drinking water, and a shrine called Lunzedi. One looks across the wooded hills and the wide brimming river, and wonders who built this Lunzedi and why. One sees in the imagination a beautiful princess looking across the river waiting for a white sail, as her heart cried out,

> "My life is dreary,
> He cometh not,
> I am aweary, aweary,
> I wish that I were dead".

So, counting the hours of sorrow, she lay the bricks to build the stupa, in memory of the one 'who cometh not': Her attendants, sharing her grief, rallied around to finish the work.

This is the kind of magic the word Lunzedi evokes in the Burmese pilgrim's mind. *Zedi* means stupa, but it is quite impossible to substitute an English word for *Lun*. This monosyllable bespeaks of grief and longing for the loved one 'who cometh not'. Lunzedi is the name given to a shrine built by someone who tried to bury a sorrow-laden heart with each brick that was laid.

Each Lunzedi has a sad story of love forsaken or lost; but this one on the slope of the hill has no story at all, either written or narrated by word of mouth. This is rather surprising in a land where almost everything of nature or human handiwork has a story.

All enquiries are met with the answer: "Oh, it's a Lunzedi ---- a Lunzedi, it is, that's all". It is rather hard on the one with unholy curiousity, and even harder for a collector of legends to resist the temptation to invent a suitable story, especially when one is under the spell of *nats,* ogres, gnomes and fairies who still exist, though unseen.

There is nothing more to be done and much less said, but to leave the Lunzedi in its quiet repose and let its silence speak eloquently of the universal story of whoever had loved and lost, and grieved in hopeless longing. The pilgrim goes onward and the enchantment of the Lunzedi gives way to new fasinations; for, one passes a few more ancient stupas, which according to the legend, were built by a *zawgyi* named Varuna.

*The story of Varuna zawgyi*

If the pilgrim's heart is touched to the core by the Lunzedi, a warm feeling of fellowship and sympathy arise as one thinks of the creator of the shrines. The pilgrim may not be enthusiastic about meeting mythical beings like ogres, but almost believes and perhaps hopes to meet a zawgyi.

Perhaps a *zawgyi* might manifest himself as on the puppet stage and in classical dramas ---dressed in red flaming robes, with a red cane in hand and dancing on light fantastic toes. He is an endearing creature, very close to the heart of the Burmese people, especially because he is so human.

*Varuna zawgyi, like all of his kind, began as a human being. He took to the woods, practised meditation, collected herbs, and did alchemy work with stones and metals. Some time later, he attained the state of zawgyi, blessed with supernormal powers and longevity of life which ran into centuries. He also enjoyed youthful appearance and vigour.*

*Varuna zawgyi dwelt for some time in the snow capped Himalavut, as the Himalaya was called then. Later he went on his wanderings, flying through the air, visiting many lands where he did alturistic works helping the good to practise the noble way of life.*

*One day, as he was air borne, he saw a long range of wooded hills along a wide brimming river, and he knew that the place was rich in magic herbs and precious stones, which would be useful to him to perfect his powers. He instantly landed on the hill top where Ponnyashin Pagoda stands today.*

*There was no pagoda at all, of course, when Varuna zawgyi first came, only seven hermits sitting in the rapture of contemplative trance. Varuna was filled with veneration when he saw the hermits sitting calm, serene, and pure like the icicles that hung on the brow of the Himalaya. Now, he thought, was his chance to do service to humanity, as that was the purpose of attaining the state of a zawgyi. He would help the hermits to practise their noble way and let their goodness and piety shine, even as a candle throws its beams in the darkness of a naughty world.*

*Varuna spread a board of fruits and drinking water for the hermits to refresh themselves when they had risen from their trance. He stayed on attending to the needs of the hermits. He made daily trips to the Himalaya, by air, of course, to get the choicest fruits. When they were sick he treated them with herbs. The seven hermits were gratified by the service Varuna gave them. They made use of the strength and health and well being to make more effort to perfect their purity and ecstasy of contemplation. This was in fact the only thing Varuna wanted. He believed that the spirit of such holy men would be the only stay for humanity.*

*An auspicious event*

*One day, it was summer and uncommonly hot. Sultry winds blustered through the woods and cruelly stripped the trees of their scanty, yellow leaves. Then suddenly something uncanny happened; the trees, bare and parched, suddenly put forth a shimmering greenery of buds and the next moment the forest was ablaze with flowers of all hues. Sweet airs that gave delight greeted the senses.*

*Even as the hermits and Varuna zawgyi stood on the hill, overcome with astonishment, they were scarcely prepared for the wonder they saw next. It was the Buddha coming airborne towards them.*

*The oldest hermit recovered himself and threw his robe on the ground for the Buddha to sit on. Then the hermits and Varuna zawgyi prostrated themselves before the Buddha. He spoke to them kindly, enquiring if they found their life in the woods too hard, if they were troubled too much by pests and beasts. The hermits answered that they were well looked after by Varuna zawgyi and they had no complaints whatsoever. The zawgyi made an umbrella of flowers and the hermits burned sweet scented herbs and listened attentively as the Buddha taught them how to practise the way to attain enlightenment.*

*The founding of Ava*

*While this was going on, an orangutan came in carrying gifts of flowers and fruits. The Buddha accepted the offertories and blessed the animal. The Buddha then stood facing the river and pointed towards a spearhead shaped promontory down south and pronounced the great future that was to be.*

*The Buddha said that this promontory, in the far off times, beyond the memory of man, had been a prosperous city and that centuries after the Buddha's time, it would again rise up in greatness and glory as a royal seat; that the orangutan who had just offered him gifts would be reborn a king there; and that the Buddha's teaching would flourish in his reign.*

*Varuna zawgyi rejoiced over the Buddha's words, feeling sure that he would live to see the kingdom of Ava rise in glory. And it was not only Varuna who rejoiced; he was joined by the nats of the hill and woods, and the whole forest rang with the triumphant applause of those beings. The fierce dragon serpents hearing the uncommon clamour, were so frightened that they burrowed deep into the ravines.*

The pilgrim looks across the river, where in the 14th century, the city of Ava was to become the royal seat; one of the wise and good kings who ruled there was Mingyiswa, who, it was believed, was the reincarnate of the orangutan who offered flowers and fruits to the Buddha.

Standing on the hill where the Buddha once stood and pronounced the words of prophecy, and thinking over the incredible events that had taken place over the ages, one feels one is being swung back and forth on a time machine. With Varuna zawgyi playing an important role in this drama of Sagaing Hills, - his life span running into years astronomical - this kind of fluctuation is to be expected.

The pilgrim looks southward and sees the hill and the ravine called today Nagashore Taung, "Dragon's Burrow", where the dragons had hidden themselves in fear. He turns his gaze east and looks on the golden pagoda on the hill overlooking the river; it is called Zetavun Pagoda, named after the hill, the habitat of the ogre chieftain named Zeta.

Varuna - a *zawgyi* - was not confined to a life of austerity and chastity. When he returned he brought with him a beautiful princess in a flower chariot.

## ZETAVUN PAGODA

*During the rejoicing over the Buddha's words of prophecy, there were yet other beings who were not frightened, instead, they were filled with wonder. They were the ogres residing on the Zeta Hill. Their chief Zeta came and requested the Buddha come to his place and speak the word of Dhamma to him and his followers.*

*So, the Buddha went to the Zeta Hill and taught the Dhamma to the ogres who attained the first stage of enlightenment, Sotapanna. The village at the foot of the hill is known today Thautarpan, the Burmese pronunciation of Sotapanna, after the ogres who attained that state.*

*Before the Buddha left, the ogresses requested the Buddha to leave something to be revered. The Buddha gave them an old robe. The ogres built a stupa and enshrined the robe therein and named it Zetavun Pagoda after their chieftain Zeta Ogre.*

*Varuna* zawgyi *stayed on with the seven hermits who practised the Buddha's Way and attained enlightenment, when they passed away they were reborn in higher celestial states. Varuna* zawgyi *went away on his wanderings. He spent some centuries at the Himalavut collecting herbs and perfecting his powers.*

The pilgrim looks at the golden Ponnyashin Pagoda and picks up the threads of the legend; the pagoda was built centuries after the Buddha's visit, when Varuna *zawgyi* had come. back from his wanderings. Varuna *zawgyi* certainly had all the time in the world.

The pilgrim - though weary - is not yet quite ready for an ascetic's life; he or she thinks wistfully of Varuna and his kind who seem to have the best of everything. Once he had attained the state of a *zawgyi,* it is not strictly necessary for him to live a life of austerity and chastity like the hermits; even as he helps the hermits to practise the way the Buddha taught, he can allow himself the pleasures of the senses.

The pilgrim remembers the stage representations of a *zawgyi's* life in classical Burmese dramas, a glamourous figure singing songs intoxicated with the beauties of nature, and dancing with flower nymphs in the forest. One also thinks of how Varuna *zawgyi* came back to the place, the very hill the pilgrim is standing on.

*Varuna returns - and departs*

*Varuna* zawgyi *did not return alone; he brought with him a beautiful princess in a flower chariot. He had found her on a desert island, where she was stranded after being shipwrecked; she and her family had to sail away from their kingdom which was invaded by barbarians. She alone survived.*

*Varuna with his supernormal powers created a great palace worthy of celestials and lived with the princess for some time, which may be reckoned in times of centuries; for the princess too, with the help of magic herbs, was also blessed with longevity of life and youth. Then some time in the 14th century of our recorded time, a son was born to the princess, and the father Varuna* zawgyi *at once knew the part his son would have to play in the future. When the boy was seven years old, he was put under a learned monk to learn the languages and the Buddhist scriptures.*

*Later, Varuna* zawgyi *and the princess had to go away; for, they had other missions to fulfill. The princess, though broken hearted to leave her son, felt her place was with her husband; and she was comforted to know that her son named Ponnya had his own work to do in the cause of the Buddha's teaching.*

## KYEEMYINTINE PAGODA

*Varuna* zawgyi *built stupas on the hill and the princess built one at the place where she used to watch her son at play on the grounds of the nearby monastery where he was being educated. The pagoda today is known as Kyeemyintine Pagoda, which means "Viewing from the High Top"*

*When the princess and Varuna* zawgyi *went away, their boy, Ponnya grew up to be a fine young man who absorbed all the learning his master the learned monk taught him. His master was a much respected teacher of the king, so Ponnya had to accompany him on his visits to the king's court. The king could not help but notice the engaging personality of the young man.*

*Ponnya was soon given a place in the king's court and he rose to be a senior minister. One day, the king received from a distant land a bejewelled gold casket; he used it as a betel casket, in which he put betel nuts, leaves and other ingredients used by addicts of betel chewing.*

*From the time the king used the casket, he became afflicted with a mysterious disease. He consulted the astrologers and they said that there must be something inside the casket that made the king ill. So the king sent for the minister Ponnya and told him to see what was wrong.*

*Ponnya took the casket home and got a goldsmith to dismantle it. Then something happened; out of the crevices of the casket came the Buddha's relics shining in a thousand iridescent colours. Ponnya and the goldsmith prostrated themselves filled with wonder and adoration.*

*Ponnya realized that donors of the casket had meant ill for the king. They had put the holy relics hidden in the casket so that the king would commit, though unwittingly, the act of desecration when he used the casket as a betel container.*

## PONNYASHIN PAGODA

*It was late in the night; there was no time to go and report to the king. So Ponnya and the goldsmith took the relics to a hill top, today known as Ponnyashin after the minister. Overnight they built a stupa with the relics enshrined in it.*

*It was Ponnya's intention to go early in the morning to the king and bring him to the stupa. But even before Ponnya could get to the king, news had already reached the palace. Some jealous people had set the king against Ponnya, insinuating that the minister had done an act of treason.*

*And, as if to testify to the statement, a resounding clamour arose; when the king opened the window to look, he saw streams of people going toward the river which was filled with boats of all sizes and shapes. The air was rent with cries of the minister's name, Ponnya, the builder of the new stupa. All the people were on their way to Ponnyashin hill, as it came to be called today.*

*The king shuddered at the thought that those people might easily be commanded to come against him and destroy him. He instantly ordered that the minister be arrested and put to death by drowning. Even as Ponnya was about to enter the palace to tell the royal master the good news of the stupa, he was met by executioners, who bound him hand and foot and took him in a boat to the middle of the river.*

*As soon as the funeral boat reached where the river was deepest, the executioners threw Ponnya into the river. That moment a miracle happened. The waters, instead of swallowing up Ponnya, circled around him in the shape of a lotus bud, and the minister was now miraculously free from his bonds.*

*The next moment all the boats carrying pilgrims to the stupa gathered round Ponnya with cries of cheer for him and vengeance for the king. Ponnya was soon taken aboard on one of the boats and all the people were at his command. Ponnya allayed their anger and made clear that he had nothing but absolute loyalty to his royal master.*

*So, finally the king heard from Ponnya's own lips the whole story of the relics enshrined in the stupa built overnight; the king, convinced of his minister's loyalty showered honours on him; Ponnya remained a trusted minister to the end of his days.*

There was one unique honour the king conferred on Ponnya. The important ritual of offering alms food at the shrine at the break of dawn - the very first offering of the day - was to be done by Ponnya and no other; not even the king should deprive him of the right.

People say that the spirit of the minister Ponnya still does his daily dawn offering of alms food at the shrine; no one has ever succeeded in offering alms food earlier than that Ponnya himself does. If you go there with your offering, before dawn, you will find that someone has been already there before you. And who else but Ponnya, now dead for these four hundred years? This is why Ponnyashin Pagoda is called Soon-oo Ponnyashin, "Shrine of the earliest dawn offering".

So this was indeed the mission Ponnya, the son of Varuna *zawgyi* and the princess, had to fulfill. Ponnyashin Pagoda is today one of the most revered shrines in the Burmese Buddhist world.

After paying respects at the Ponnyashin Shrine, the pilgrim goes down the foot path shaded with champac trees, toward Zetavun Pagoda, built by the ogres tamed by the Buddha. Before he takes a boat up north, he looks toward the village called Yewunn, "Encircling Waters", named to mark the place where the minister Ponnya, thrown into the river, was seen afloat amidst circling waters.

When the minister Ponnya was thrown into the river, the waters split and formed a circle around him.

The minister was always the first to make the dawn offering at the shrine - a tradition that lives on to this day.

# CHAPTER VIII

# MOUNT POPA: THE ABODE OF GODS

The traveller going north up the Irrawaddy River looks upon the panorama of varying landscape of the picturesque river valley, with ridges of hills in the far background, and rather arid, rolling hills as one progresses into the "Dry Zone" of Central Burma. Just when one begins to feel the monotony of the general contours, a unique sight suddenly emerges.

There, rising above the range of hills is Mount Popa. It stands completely alone, above the low ridges of sandstone, sparsely scattered over the countryside. The awesome grandeur of its steep sides and craggy top are tempered by wisps of feathery clouds that lace and flounce along the stern precipices.

Mount Popa is an extinct volcano, situated 40 miles southeast of Pagan, Burma's ancient city and living treasure-house of Buddhist architectural beauties.

Even from afar, Mount Popa casts its spell on travellers cruising up and down the Irrawaddy. Like all marvels of nature, Popa fulfils the need of the people, spiritual as well as intellectual. If the great mountain's overwhelming majesty awakens the lyrical in the heart, its baffling mystery challenges the mind to explore it.

The highway to Popa runs from Pagan through the arid dusty plains, relieved occasionally by toddy palm groves, where one can buy jaggery sweets packed in neat dry palm leaf boxes. As the mountain looms near, the dry lands give way to rich vineyards, banana plantations and lush woodland interlaced with gushing streams.

*Taungkalat*

The two places of interest are the main volcano, and what is known as Taungkalat, which is an unfilled neck or plug of a subsidiary volcano. It is an isolated peak, extremely precipitous; its shape suggests to the Burmese an antique tray that rests on a single stem, *kalat,* as it is called. One

Mount Popa, the abode of *nats* in the woodlands---an enchanted place where goblins and spirits still wander. Like all marvels of nature, Mount Popa fulfils the needs of the people, spiritual as well as intellectual.

can drive right up to the base of Taungkalat, where ample parking space and guest-houses are available.

Part of the ascent to the peak is a stone-paved pathway gradually rising almost imperceptibly until it reaches a steep climb. From there is a stairway that runs up to the top.

On the top are pagodas and Buddhist shrines. The view of the country-side from there is breath-taking.

All the way up, small monkeys keep company with the pilgrims. They are very tame, used to being fed with bananas. There is no danger from them, except that one's sun-glasses and hats may be swooped away by their pilfering fingers.

### *The Main Volcano of Mount Popa*

A recently built stairway leads all the way up the main volcano, but not many attempt the climb. The mountain rises to 4981 feet above sea level. Mount Popa was originally a circular crater, but the whole of the northern side has been blown away. The present mountain is in the shape of a horse-shoe.

The main mountain looks like an ordinary volcano with conical silhouette and concave slopes, steepest near the crater rim. The crater wall inside is precipitous, often with steep cliffs with drops of a thousand feet.

Once a year there is a large outing organized, and thousands of pilgrims make the journey to the top at that time.

### *Abode of Nats*

Mount Popa with its sylvan surroundings is an enchanted place for the Burmese, dating back to pre-Buddhist days. It was and still is, the abode of deities of all levels and shapes, represented in sculptures in the area. Now that most of the deities have become Buddhists, along with their worshippers, the descendants of the original worshippers give respect and reverence as guardians of the family.

It is meet that the chief deity of Mount Popa, once a flaming volcano, should be the spirit of a blacksmith of fabulous strength. When he struck the gigantic hammer on the anvil, the thundering sound crashed all over the countryside; then followed the burst of flames from his forge that looked as hell's fires had risen out of the earth.

The name of the deity is "Min Mahagiri", "Lord of the Great Mountain". From his exalted throne of Mount Popa, he holds sway over every family "who has a roof over the head", according to the legend.

One of the items sold at fruit-shops everywhere in this country is fresh green coconut with the stem intact; each coconut is encased in a woven cane hanger decorated with a spray of red ribbon and a long-stemmed palm leaf fan. This ensemble of a green coconut, red ribbon and fan is used for offering to "Lord of the Great Mountain", who is also the guardian of the household. The offering is placed in a special niche in the homes where old customs still prevail. This offering for the guardian of the household is always placed lower than the household shrine where the Buddha statue is.

The families who do not actually observe the ritual of offering the green coconut and its accessories, recognize the presence of the household guardian by remembering him in the daily devotions at the household shrine; this assures him that he has the family's goodwill and loving kindness, and most important of all, that he is called upon to rejoice in the good deeds the family does, by which act the guardian spirit will gain a share of the merit gained.

The offering of green coconut and fan is a meaningful gesture; it is a sympathetic offering to the one who died in fire. Coconut juice is considered a relief for burns. This has to do with the story of Lord of the Great Mountain in his previous life as a man, before he became a spirit. The story began at Tagaung, an ancient city up north on the Irrawaddy.

*A Blacksmith of Tagaung and his two sisters*

The ancient city of Tagaung is considered one of the roots of Burmese history, and it dates back to the pre-Buddhist days. At that time there lived a young blacksmith, comely of face and strong of body. Loved and admired for his good looks and strength, which was said to be the strength of five elephants, he lived with his two young sisters, Dway Hla and Dway Phyu.

*Maung Tint Dai (Mr. Handsome), for that was the blacksmith's name, was popular with people and they loved to tell stories of how he could break the tusk of a raging elephant. This was hardly the kind of thing to please a reigning king of those times.*

*In the young blacksmith the king saw a potential threat to his power and security. He was determined to put him out of the way.*

*The king's attempts to capture the young blacksmith met with something less than success. Maung Tint Dai's loyal friends and elders of his village protected him by giving timely warnings of the king's men's forays. His haunts in the woodlands where he had to spend most of his time, burning charcoal, were good hideouts. His two young sisters were also well looked after by the elders of the village.*

*The king's unseemly conduct*

*One day the king was touring the country and he passed the village where the blacksmith's sisters lived. The king saw the beautiful Dway Hla and he was smitten by her modesty and charm. The king took the girl back to the royal city and made her his chief consort.*

*Coming home from hiding, the young blacksmith heard what had happened. In a society where taking a girl without the consent of her parents or guardians was an offence, it was a great dishonour on the part of the family so transgressed. King or commoner, no one could do such a thing to his family. He had to show his dissent somehow.*

*The irate brother shows his dissent*

*So the young blacksmith took his gigantic hammer and struck it on the anvil with such might that the earth quaked beneath the blow and the king himself was jolted from his royal seat.*

*Dway Hla knew immediately that it must be her irate brother's doing. She had to admit to the king that she was the sister of the man the king hated so much. She begged forgiveness and amnesty for her brother now that they were bound by family ties.*

*Shaken badly by the thunderous sound of the young blacksmith's hammer, and the discovery that his beloved queen was the sister of his bitterest adversary, the king appreciated the situation well enough to use it to his own advantage.*

*The king makes a devious plan*

*The king acted pleased; why was he not told this before? He had always meant to take the young blacksmith to his court and give him a high place; it was not every king who had a man of such strength and courage to serve him; and to think that he was his own brother-in-law. He surely owed an apology to the head of the family of which he was a member now.*

*The young queen was persuaded to send a message to her brother telling him to come straight to the court to be honoured.*

*Maung Tint Dai was overjoyed to receive the message. He had implicit faith in the king's*

Dway Hla threw herself into the burning fire to prove her innocence and loyalty to her brother.

*word and he trusted his sister, who would wish nothing but good for him.*

*Therefore, he could hardly believe his eyes when, on arriving at the royal city, he was confronted by a group of armed men, who instantly bound him hand and foot and led him to a huge Sagar tree; at the foot of the tree was a pile of faggots, his funeral pyre.*

*A sister's grief*

*Dway Hla was all the time waiting to welcome her brother whose finest hour she longed to share. As she waited and waited, one of her attendants brought the news of her brother's fate. Mad with grief she ran out of the palace, her long hair flying in the wind, her dress all awry.*

*She ran ahead of her attendants who tried to catch up with her, until she reached the foot of the tree where the executioners had just begun to put flaming torches to the pyre of faggots.*

*Sobbing and wailing, she let forth words begging forgiveness of her brother; and to prove her innocence and loyalty, she threw herself into the burning pyre. Her attendants tried to pull her away but they only caught her long hair and her beautiful face was all they managed to save. Her spirit thus came to be known as Golden Face.*

*The huge tree where the brother and sister were burnt to death, became the abode of their spirits. It so happened that the king was not to be spared the ill repute of his treachery and cruelty. One of the popular ditties sung by the people at the time runs something like this, featuring the name of the blacksmith Tint Dai:*

O Tint Dai, Tint Dai, poor simple Tint
Dai, Strong and brawny and brave
was he,
Trusting, trusting and trusting, poor Tint
Dai, Saw not the king's duplicity.

*The tree where the brother and sister met their death became a symbol of the king's treachery.*

*Down to the city of Pagan*

*Later, the king ordered that the tree should be uprooted and thrown into the river Irrawaddy. The tree floated down the river and reached the city of Pagan, then a rising city state. With the tree also came the story of the tragic death of the simple blacksmith and his sister.*

*People were deeply moved by the blacksmith's tragic death and his sister's devotion and the story reached the ear of the then reigning king of Pagan. The King personally came in state to the river bank where the Sagar tree came to rest.*

*It was then the spirits of the brother and sister appeared before the king and told their story, and begged for a place to live. The King of Pagan in his compassion granted that the brother and sister should find a home "under any roof" that sheltered a family. By this edict they became virtually the guardians of every household.*

The people, already touched by the story, welcomed the king's orders by offering a green coconut and fan and flowers in honour of the spirits of the brother and sister, a tradition which lives to this day.

By the king's grace, the young blacksmith and his sister made their permanent home on Mount Popa, and he became known as Lord of the Great Mountain, his sister as the Golden Face. They were later joined by their youngest surviving sister Dway Phyu, who died of a broken heart.

*Maung Tint Dai's mistress*

*It so happened that as a young blacksmith, Maung Tint Dai, during his long years of wandering in the woodlands, had met a girl named Shwe Nabay. She was a water-serpent girl who with her super-normal powers could take human form. In the shape of a comely maid she haunted the streams and lakes of the woodlands, and there, met the young blacksmith.*

MIN MAHAGIRI - "Lord of the Great Mountain", the Popa *nat.*

*Hot and tired with his wanderings and with baking charcoal in the woods, Maung Tint Dai found solace in the cool refreshing embrace of the amphibian maid. Their baby girl was barely a toddler when the young blacksmith met his fate at the hands of the king. The mother died soon after the news reached her.*

*Ma Nai Lay ("Little Miss Lonesome") was the name given to the orphan girl, who was not too long in joining her parents on Mount Popa.*

### *The Peter Pan of the Pantheon of Spirits*

Little Miss Lonesome was the Peter Pan of the pantheon of spirits. She stayed a child to this day. She is represented as a child in the cradle. At the ritual feasts, when the medium is possessed by her spirit, she speaks in the lisping voice of a child and she is a great favourite with the Burmese people.

When there is a new baby in the family, offerings are made to Little Miss Lonesome. The offering is simple, a plate of freshly cooked rice, seasoned with sessamum oil and a hard-boiled egg. The plate is put at the head of the cradle of the new baby.

Little Miss Lonesome is also a playmate of babies. When a baby smiles, people say, "Little Miss Lonesome is teasing it". And when the baby cries, people remonstrate: "Oh please, Little Miss Lonesome, don't tease the baby too much; please make it smile again".

Little Miss Lonesome is considered a good friend of young people, who often call upon her to help with their affairs. Gifts of tiny slippers and small dresses, like the doll's wardrobe, are offered at her shrine with the incantation like "Please send Mr. Right soon". This little Peter Pan of the pantheon is a solace to lonely hearts and her shrine is a haven for the love-lorn.

*Part of the people's life*

Spirits or deities are real people, and they are very much a part of the human's everyday life. To be in the vicinity of Mount Popa means to be emotionally involved with the deities, spirits and mythical beings - more often than not, in spite of oneself.

It is not quite possible to deny the presence of spirits and deities, as they have a way of manifesting themselves, that is, by making people talk of them as if they were real living things. People refer to them as natually as they would talk of a respected elder of the community. People speak of them with deep respect, nay, not in fear, but in loving kindness. They are the people's friends, though unseen, as one might suppose, but whose presence is genuinely felt and experienced.

*More deities, more stories*

Around Popa are shrines for many other deities. In one of the shrines is a statue of a lady; her face is beautiful; she wears a head-dress, a mask of an ogress, protruding eyes and knotted fangs. Her name is Golden Girl, called respectfully as Popa Mother. She is an ogress-nymph living on flowers.

Before going on with her story, here is a forty-year-old pop song, still popular today:

Popa, the Sacred Mount Popa,
The Golden Popa, how I wish I could come to thee.
How I wish I could be where in their grand shrine,
Dwell happy the Blacksmith Maung Tint Dai
And his sisters.
O how I wish to be where the dark stranger Byatta,
With his Golden Girl went a mating,
And where their two princely sons came forth.

SHWE MYETNA - "Golden Face", Min Mahagiri's elder sister who also is one of the seven Mt. Popa *nats*.

Little Miss Lonesome, the Peter Pan of the pantheon of Burmese nats. Losing her parents, she was left alone. Later she joined her parents, the Popa Nats. She is the patron *nat* and playmate of children. When there is a new baby in the family, an offering of boiled egg is put at the head of the cradle as an offering to her.

Mount Popa is also associated with the name Byatta, the dark stranger who came over this land from across the sea; he was a trusted henchman of King Anawrahta, who reigned in Pagan in the Eleventh Century A.D. His mistress, the Golden Girl, had two sons: Min Gyi and Min Lay, the most well-known in the pantheon of spirits.

Their story is a patchwork of history, legend and myth. The two sons of Popa Mother represent the worst, as well as the best, of an age --- an age of reckless gallantry when power, gold and women were won at the point of the sword. Min Gyi and Min Lay were executed by the order of the king, who later granted them permission to hold sway over the village of Taungpyone, near Mandalay.

At Taungpyone an annual festival in honour of Min Gyi and Min Lay is held in the month of July. It is generally regarded as an occasion for unrestrained merry-making where people just let themselves go in boisterous drinking and dancing. Perhaps it is an annual "letting off steam" for all kinds of people.

The full story of Min Gyi and Min Lay has been spun into the story of Mandalay.

Mount Popa, the abode of the gods amidst the woodlands, is an enchanted place where goblins and spirits still wander. There is a being called *zawgyi,* one of the mythical characters represented on the Burmese stage; he is dressed in flaming red robes, wears a red cap, and has a magic wand in his hand.

The *zawgyi* is a human being who has attained miraculous powers, one of which is long life and youthfulness. He is supposed to have attained such powers by concocting something out of the herbs grown in the Mount Popa area. The Burmese indigenous medicine men believe that the herbs which grow in the Popa area have more potency than those grown elsewhere. In many ways, therefore, to be around Mount Popa means to get involved in a multi-coloured mesh of religious faith, ancient rites and jungle lore, with mythical beings popping in and out like well-meaning but interfering neighbours.

Do not for a moment think that it would be easy to sort yourself out of this labyrinth of legends and normal living. It would take some time to be back in the worrisome workaday world.

*

# CHAPTER IX

# KYAITIYO

*An exhilarating journey into a land of fantasy*

Kyaiktiyo - the name spells magic, fantasy and spiritual exultation to the Burmese Buddhists, among whom the conversation often leads to the question: "Have you been to Kyaiktiyo yet?". It means: "You haven't really lived until you've been there". Among the Sino-Burmese, to have been there three times means a realisation of a life dream, and also a lifetime of blessedness and prosperity.

Kyaiktiyo pagoda is about 18 feet high, built on a huge boulder 50 feet in girth, that rests precariously on a projecting tabular rock 80 feet high, which itself is separated several feet from the mountain edge by a deep chasm. It is an overwhelming sight to the Buddhists, not only as a marvel of nature, but also as a grand manifestation of their ancestors' faith in the teachings of the Buddha.

The area was known in the ancient days as Suvannabhumi or the Golden Land. It lies to the north of what is known as the Tenasserim. It is a coastal strip with its back to the mountain ranges along the peninsula which is shared by the southwest tip of Thailand and by Malaysia. It is where the two missionary monks Shin Sona and Shin Uttara landed after a perilous journey from India. Suvannabhumi is picturesque country; rain forests and mountains on one side and the seashore lined with thousands of islands on the other.

To the non-Burmese, the trip is exhilarating; the journey by train or car from Rangoon, 100 miles along the greenery of woods and paddy fields, includes a crossing over the Sittang river by a beautiful suspension bridge 2,311 feet long. The first stop is Kyaikto, a small town, from where a bus route, nine miles long, leads to a base camp called Kinpun at the foot of the mountain ridge.

Kyaiktiyo Pagoda as seen today, one of the holy places for Burmese Buddhist pilgrims.

There begins a seven and a half mile stretch of mountain scrambling through the lush rain forests, towering hills and rippling streams. Once the pilgrims reach Kinpun base camp, they see shrines with larger-than-life sculptures of nats, in the shape of venerable gentlemen in elegant old-style ceremonial costumes of silk, attended by monstrous-looking ogres and ferocious tigers.

From Kinpun camp, pilgrims begin their journey uphill. The place is a hubbub of activity, a wide stretch of woodlands of leafy trees and meadows, laced with cool clear springs. It is a welcome rest to the tired traveller. There, under the spreading trees, bullock carts stand at ease, propped on their shafts while the cattle graze nearby. There are *zayats* or rest-houses where pilgrims may rest before their climb. *Zayats* are built by donors and pilgrims are under no obligation to pay anything for using them. Any contribution toward the upkeep is voluntary.

*Festivals -- and con-men*

During the festival season (October to March), the base camp is a trade fair. The long line of bamboo and thatch huts is an exotic bazaar where vendors from all parts of the country display their wares, mostly handicrafts, useful decorative things in cane, bamboo and reeds. There are also medicinal herbs and animal products like horns, claws and bones.

There are things that the Burmese traditional lore recommends for home cures: for instance, tiger's milk, bile of boa-constrictor, tiger's claws, and animal horns. Tiger's claws worn round an infant's neck are protection against infantile ills; tiger's milk acts as immunisation against infections, so does the bile of boa-constrictor. It is within reason that things like claws, horns and bile can be obtained but, how on earth does anyone get tiger's milk? Can anyone, with all the ingenuity humans are capable of, ever milk a tigress? We are enlightened, on this point, by the jungle lore which says that mama tigress, because of the roughness of her cubs' tongues, cannot bear to be sucked: so she lets her milk fall on leaves for her young to lap up. Tiger cubs, it appears, are not breast-fed like other mammals.

Chances are that pilgrims will fall victim to con-men. I still remember with amusement an incident that happened to us many years ago while on a trip to Kyaiktiyo pagoda. Our party was scrambling up the hill when a rough-looking hill-billy came out of a nearby thicket. He carried a basket on his shoulder; in the basket was the huge coil of a dead boa. We were very excited to meet a boa hunter in person; here was a chance to get genuine boa bile. We stopped the man to ask, but he was not very communicative, only eager to be off. He did not seem to understand what we said and he spoke a dialect with only a sprinkling of Burmese words. It was some time before he reluctantly produced a few small sacs with black substance in them. One Mr. Know-all in our party said that it was, indeed, genuine boa bile. Then followed another fifteen minutes of gibberish and gesticulations. Finally, we did manage to get the sacs - for a good price. When the man left, Mr. Know-all said the poor man did not really know the real worth of his wares. I felt guilty for having swindled the man.

Only when we showed off our acquisitions to the local people did we realise who it was that was swindled. We had been treated to a rare exhibition of showmanship: the dead boa in a basket; the man's sinister look; his reluctance to speak and some gibberish. We had a good laugh at ourselves. I almost thought the man really had earned his money. It was a good show and we certainly paid a good price for it. If the con-men make an easy (or is it that easy?) living, there are others, who really earn it with the sweat of their brows - the porters and carriers. Porters carry the pilgrims' luggage, and the carriers the pilgrims who are unwilling or unable to make the long climb on foot.

Children are carried in cane baskets hanging from poles flung over the carriers' shoulders. Adults go up in hammocks, a strong cotton blanket tied lengthwise to a bamboo pole and carried by two men. It looks a nice ride; some even read a paper or a book. So, children and adults swing along merrily up the hill as others scramble up no less cheerily.

People usually begin their journey in the cool hours of the afternoon and, as the darkening twilight closes in, bamboo torches light the way up. There are many stop-overs on the way where the forbidding inclinations give way to kinder slopes. There is a hut or two, where vendors sell things to chew. Some of the climbs are quite steep and challenging, especially to the residents of the flat-lands. They have expressive names like "Shew-yin-so" ("Heaving Chest") and "Pho-pyan-taung" ("Old-Man-Turns-Back-Hill"). There is a flow of pilgrims going up or down the path. Those coming down hail the up comers with words of encouragement; "Come on, the pagoda is just ahead," or "You are doing fine - keep it up". At one of the stops, called "Myin-daw-mu" ("The View") pilgrims have a glimpse of the Kyaiktiyo pagoda - something really exhilarating. The pilgrims then are convinced the trip was worth everything they had gone through. There, telescopes are available on hire.

After three miles of trudging, the pilgrims come to "Yay-myaung-gyi" ("Big Stream Camp"). There again are *zayats* where pilgrims may refresh themselves. Food and snacks and soft drinks are available at the shops. The highlight of the place is the deep, wide stream brimming with cool clear water, wherein pilgrims may dip. There are bath houses, complete with mirrors and *thanakha* bark and stone slabs to grind on. The *thanakha* paste, cool and fragrant, is a must in the Burmese ladies' beauty ritual.

*The legend*

Yaymyaunggyi has a magic of its own, for it was here that a young queen, Shwenankyin, stopped on her way back from her husband's palace to her parents' home. She was the daughter of a highland chief and King Tissa had fallen in love with her while he was in the locality building the Kyaiktiyo pagoda, two thousand years ago.

*It was the custom of Shwenankyin's family to make offerings to the family guardian* nat *on occasions like marriage. In the fuss and excitement of the royal favour, they forgot the traditional ritual. The king took the girl to his kingdom to be his queen. Later, Shwenankyin became pregnant and was sick most of the time. Her father heard of her illness and decided that it must be due to their failure to make the offering to the family* nat. *He went to the royal city and asked the king's permission to take his daughter home so she could offer apologies and ritual offerings to the* nat. *The king, though he did not quite believe the queen's sickness was due to the* nat's *anger, thought it wise not to go against the tribal customs of his subjects. And it would not do to have his young wife obsessed with superstitious fears.*

*So, Shwenankyin went along with her father. It was a long journey through the untamed forests. By the time they reached the "Big Stream Camp", they had lost most of their retinue through sickness or in the jaws of wild beasts. There were only three of them; Shwenankyin, her father and her brother.*

*The family* nat *now felt the family was within his power. He instantly set his tiger on them. As the tiger shot out of the thicket, Shwenankyin's father and brother ran for their lives, leaving her alone. Heavy with child, Shwenankyin felt the only refuge would be the contemplation of the Buddha's infinite compassion. She looked toward the Kyaiktiyo pagoda, wherein her royal spouse had enshrined the Buddha's hair and surrendered herself to her fate.*

*The tiger retreated into the jungle leaving Shwenankyin unharmed. Separated from her brother and her father, she went on her journey until she came to the pagoda platform. Exhausted but filled with the ecstatic joy of looking on the pagoda, and contemplating the Buddha's attributes, she happily laid herself to rest -- forever.*

*Before she took her final breath, Shwenankyin made a wish to be near the pagoda for all time: she prayed that her body would never be removed from the place. When her sorrowing husband and relatives came to bury her, they found the body had turned to stone. Today, a shrine is erected to her memory. Her spirit is still there. She has become a* nat *that radiates love and goodness.*

The pilgrims are helped along by good *nats* like Shwenankyin who lives in the memory of men and women and whose spirit rejoices in their good deeds. All round are layers of hills and ridges, the hill tops floating like islets in the sea of billowy mists.

According to the legend, the pagoda was built by King Tissa, 2500 years ago. The building of the pagoda was no small feat. It could not have been done but for the help and support of *nats*. In this case, that of no less a *nat* than Thagyarmin, king of *nats*, who came down from the lofty regions to make things possible.

*King Tissa's birth is a fantastic story. His father was a demi-god or* Zawgyi, *whose figure we see today on the puppet stage, a glamorous being resplendent in flaming robes. His mother belongs to the race of* nagas, *a kind of* nat *whose shape is a serpent and whose habitat was the sea;* nagas *with their godly powers can change themselves into any shape they wish.*

*One day a* naga *girl, who had lost her loved one, came to the human abode. She took the shape of a beautiful maid and wandered in the woodlands. There was a demi-god who lived in a cave near a hermitage. He was a disciple of the hermit whom he revered. He went daily to the hermitage and gave the hermit his personal service. The* naga *girl saw and fell in love with him. She was not sure how he would respond to her advances. Maybe he did not care for such pleasures, having the hermit as his mentor. So she went into his cave, while he was away at the hermitage, and made a beautiful bed of fragrant flowers. She hid herself nearby to see what would happen. If the demi-god threw away the flowers, he must be above such pleasures.*

*Things went well. The demi-god enjoyed the flowery bed and the* naga *girl, too. They lived happily. One day the girl laid an egg. Out of the egg grew a boy who was reared as the hermit's own son. One day, the people of the hermit's former kingdom came and asked him to come back and be king. The hermit, having no wish to do so, gave the boy to them to rule the kingdom, which prospered under him.*

*Tissa became a great king and he often went to pay his respects to the hermit. One day, the hermit sent for him and told him how once the Buddha himself had come to this land and had given him a tress of hair, which he had kept in his own hair-knot. Now that his end was near, he wanted it to be enshrined in a stupa. One of the conditions he wanted was that Tissa must find a rock which looked exactly like his head. On such a rock, a shrine must be built to receive the Buddha's hair.*

*It was a cue for Thagyarmin, king of* nats, *to come down and help. He scoured the boundless sea beds to look for a stone that looked like the hermit's cranium. He found one and the king, feeling he had to do his part in the great deed, asked Thagyarmin to allow him to carry the stone in his ship. The stone, the one on which the pagoda stands enshrining the Buddha's hair, was taken on the king's ship. As soon as the rock was placed on the precipice, the ship turned into stone because, after carrying such a sacred object, no lesser cargo must be allowed to defile the vessel. There, on the stoned shaped like a boat, stand "Kyauk-than-ban" pagoda, ("Stone Boat" pagoda).*

King Tissa and his Karen queen, adoring Kyaiktiyo Pagoda.

*Around the Pagoda*

The story, fantastic as it is, is as real as if it had happened only a short time ago. All around the environs of the pagoda are testimonies. There is a cave whose entrance is shaped like a crow's beak. There are Buddha images in there. Perhaps not quite appropriately, for the place was the scene of romance between the naga girl and the demi-god. It was in there that the naga made an inviting floral bed exotically scented to seduce the demi-god.

There are hills with names like Yatha Taung ("the Hermit's Hill") and Mokesoh Taung ("the Hunter's Hill"). The cup-like marks on a stone slab tell the story of how a hunter, on meeting the hermit, knelt in respect and how he left his calling to become a good disciple. The 'cups' on the stone slab show where his knees rested.

There are springs and waterholes whose waters are believed to cure ills. People take the water home in bottles. To the north of the "Hunter's Hill" are twin pagodas built on a massive stone slab. There are gold leaf vendors who also do the gilding which, in itself, is a breathtaking feat. The vendor takes the gold leaves and crosses to the stone slab, on which the pagodas stand, by means of a rope flung across a gap one hundred feet wide and fifty feet above ground. The vendor hangs on to the rope with his hands and moves along, alternating his hands to move forward. He comes back the same way.

About a mile away from the "Twin Pagodas", there is another set of twin pagodas, called the "Naga-paya" ("the Serpent Pagoda") and "Pha-paya", (the "Frog Pagoda"). These pagodas commemorate an event which happened during the lifetime of the hermit, according to the legend.

*One day a serpent was chasing a frog until they came to the environs of the hermitage. So great was the hermit's power of loving kindness that the two stopped in their tracks, the predator without any desire to hurt, and the prey without fear.*

It is impossible to be in the vicinity of the Kyaiktiyo Pagoda or any pagoda in Burma, and not be emotionally involved. There are the hermits full of loving kindness and virtue, the *naga* girl in search of romance, the demi-gods full of the joy of life, the *nats*, both good and bad, and the all-powerful Thagyarmin, king of the *nats,* to put things right.

There's fantasy, magic and adventure and very little, if any, history, -- but who minds?

*

## THE AUTHOR

Khin Myo Chit, born 1915, started writing short stories in Burmese in the *Dagon Magazine* in 1934. She worked on the editorial staff of *The Burma Journal* during the years when the country seethed with anti-colonial movements for national independence, and after the war, on a Burmese newspaper *The Oway.*

She graduated from the University of Rangoon in 1952 and served as Features Editor in *The Guardian Daily* when she began writing short stories and articles in English. "The 13 Carat Diamond" appeared first in *The Guardian Magazine,* and was included in *"Fifty Great Oriental Stories"* published in The United States and Canada. It was also translated into German, Italian, Gujarati and Yugoslav. Another short story, "Her Infinite Variety", won a Horizons Prize in a contest among Asian countries. "The Four Puppets", a folk tale, was published in *"Folk Tales of Asia",* sponsored by the Asian Cultural Centre for UNESCO.

Her English publications include *Burmese Scenes and Sketches* and *Colourful Burma,* the latter being an enlarged edition of her short stories and articles. "Quest for Peace", which was serialized in *The Working People's Daily* while she was on the staff of that paper, is largely autobiographical. *"Anawrahta of Burma"* is a historical novel based on the life of King Anawrahta, the 11th Century founder of the first Burmese Kingdom with its capital Pagan.

She was awarded the Mawgun (Independence) Medal in 1983 for her patriotic work during Burma's Independence struggle, and continues writing both in Burmese and English.

## THE ARTIST

Paw Oo Thet was born in 1936, at Mandalay, the undisputed seat of Burmese culture. His father was a well known artist. From the age of fifteen, Paw Oo Thet received his training under excellent professional artists of the time. At twenty, he was already working as a designer at a textile printing factory. Later he worked as a full time cartoonist on the staff of a leading newspaper. In 1960 he won an American Scholarship that enabled him to take a correspondence course from F.A.S. (Famous Artists School). He contributed to the UNICEF calendars and diaries of 1965, 1975, 1982, 1983. He is also one of the founders of the Lokanat Art Gallery in Rangoon, established in 1972. Recently he has won one of the special prizes in the B.B.C. Jubilee Art Competition. Paw Oo Thet has had many shows of his works in Mandalay and Rangoon, and is one of the best known and loved artists in contemporary Burma.